His Power Through You

by Charles ♥ Frances Hunter

Published by HUNTER BOOKS
201 McClellan Road
Kingwood, Texas 77339

BOOKS BY CHARLES ♥ FRANCES HUNTER

A CONFESSION A DAY KEEPS THE DEVIL AWAY
ANGELS ON ASSIGNMENT
ARE YOU TIRED?
BORN AGAIN! WHAT DO YOU MEAN?
COME ALIVE
DON'T LIMIT GOD
FOLLOW ME
GOD IS FABULOUS
GOD'S ANSWER TO FAT...LOØSE IT!
GOD'S CONDITIONS FOR PROSPERITY
HIS POWER THROUGH YOU
HOT LINE TO HEAVEN
HOW TO MAKE YOUR MARRIAGE EXCITING
IF YOU REALLY LOVE ME...
IMPOSSIBLE MIRACLES
IT'S SO SIMPLE (formerly HANG LOOSE WITH JESUS)
LET'S GO WITNESSING (formerly GO, MAN, GO)
MEMORIZING MADE EASY
MY LOVE AFFAIR WITH CHARLES
NUGGETS OF TRUTH
POSSESSING THE MIND OF CHRIST
P.T.L.A. (Praise the Lord, Anyway!)
SIMPLE AS A.B.C.
SINCE JESUS PASSED BY
the fabulous SKINNIE MINNIE RECIPE BOOK
SUPERNATURAL HORIZONS (from Glory to Glory)
THE DEVIL WANTS YOUR MIND
THE TWO SIDES OF A COIN
THIS WAY UP!
TO HEAL THE SICK
WHY SHOULD "I" SPEAK IN TONGUES???

ISBN 0-917726-74-X

Scripture quotations are taken from:
The Authorized King James Version (KJV).
The Living Bible, Paraphrased (TLB), ©1971 by Tyndale House Publishers, Wheaton, Il.
The New King James Version (NKJV), ©1979, 1980, 1982 by Thomas Nelson, Inc., Nashville, Tn.
Revised Standard Version ©1946, 1952 by Division of Christian Education of the NCCC, U.S.A., and used by permission.

TABLE OF CONTENTS

His Power Through You

In the event your Christian Bookstore does not have any of the books written by Charles and Frances Hunter or published by Hunter Books, please write for price list and order blank from HUNTER BOOKS.

For additional information on how to have a Video Healing School in your church or Bible study group, write to:

HUNTER MINISTRIES
201 McClellan Road
Kingwood, Texas 77339, U.S.A

Chapter One

Jesus Speaks to His People

"Suddenly a brilliant light from heaven spotted down upon him! He fell to the ground and heard a voice saying to him, 'Paul! Paul! Why are you persecuting me'

"'Who is speaking, sir?' Paul asked.

"And the voice replied, 'I am Jesus, the one you are persecuting! Now get up and go into the city and await my further instructions'" (Acts 9:4-6 TLB).

by Frances

Just as Jesus appeared to Paul on the road to Damascus, He appeared in person at our Campmeeting '83 during one of the afternoon services. Those attending that service will never be the same again. It occurred during high praise and worship.

The dramatic appearance was preceded by a huge super white cloud on the stage which covered the entire area and looked like a huge thunderhead in the sky. The glory and the presence of God was immediately felt...the very air seemed to be charged with electricity. There was a stillness and a holiness that you could almost reach out and touch! The effect was so awesome it was impossible to speak or to hear because to be in the presence of the Lord Jesus Christ is almost more than a human mind or body can stand.

After a few brief moments, He disappeared back into the glory cloud, and my heart cried out, "Jesus come back! Come back! Don't go away!" He had literally melted into the glory of God and was not visible for any of us to see.

Suddenly, as quickly as He had disappeared, He seemed to walk back through the cloud of God's presence and was again visible. Our hearts raced with excitement and joy! The pleasure of the moment was savored and relished by everyone who saw the vision, however, the glory of the moment was short-lived because once again He seemed to just dissolve into the glory of God and was no longer visible. Again my inner being cried out, "Don't go away, Jesus! Don't go away, Jesus! Don't go away, Jesus! Come back! Come back!" No one who has ever beheld Jesus will ever want to depart from His presence. I knew He was there, but I couldn't see Him because He was hidden in God's glory!

His appearance and then His disappearance into the glory cloud continued for possibly twelve to fifteen minutes, and then GOD SPOKE! He said, "This is the way I want YOU to be. I want you to be so hidden in Him that the world will never see you, but all they will see is My glory!"

God wants us to be walking in the beauty of His holiness so all that people will be able to see is His glory, and nothing of our earthly selves. He is calling on the body of Christ to be so totally committed to Him that nothing else matters in our lives and that we will be so "in Him" that the world will see Jesus in us.

Jesus is calling for a holy people to be so caught up in the things of God that Paul's statement, "I am in the world, but not *of* the world" will become a reality in all of our lives.

Jesus verified this truth to us when He appeared during the summer of 1984 at the Convention Center in Fresno, this time to Charles. Charles shared the vision with the audience as soon as Jesus appeared, and as it was actually happening.

by Charles

As I stood there, I saw Jesus clearly and distinctly as though He was standing right in front of me. His feet stood on the floor and His head was at the top of the auditorium. Angels stood guard as though they had their spears on either side. There were movements around Him of others from heaven.

I could not take my eyes off of the center of Jesus. I began to see the people in the auditorium as everyone began to truly enter into Spirit worship, into the very presence of God.

Jesus said, "When you enter into Me, it's as if you've already raptured to that extent." I could see the people in front of Him were suddenly rapturing up into Him, not outside of the building but rapturing up into Jesus Himself. They were literally zooming up and dissolving into Him instead of standing down on the floor.

The height and breadth of the auditorium was like the whole heaven and earth. Jesus was filling all of it as though He stood in the center of all creation, all of heaven, all of the universe. Instead of just filling this building, He filled the whole universe.

I saw that Jesus wants this earth filled with His glory. As the worship began, the room began to fill with the glory cloud. It was like a smoke filled room, a blueness, a pureness that came forth. This haze preceded the coming of Jesus into the room, into the whole dominion that we occupied.

Then I saw the earth upon which He stood. I saw Him in as great a proportion and size upon the earth as one would think of Him in the building from top to bottom. He stood upon the whole earth. Not upon one spot, but as the earth rotated, He was all over the whole earth. He wants the earth to be covered with His glory and we do think of Him as covering all of the earth. His cloud of glory covers the entire earth.

With this glory, He wants to cover the whole earth and as we're rapturing up into Him, He also comes down to us. Not at the end of time, but now, today. He comes into us and He disperses Himself into the multitudes of people who are yielding totally to Him.

Then I saw this awesome huge Jesus descend and disappear into each of us in the audience.

We became full of the Lord Jesus Christ, full of His glory and full of His might as we moved across the earth and multiplied ourselves until all the people of the earth knew Him. He comes into us and His glory fills the earth just as the waters cover the sea. He is totally in us.

In these last days, I see this is coming forth very, very soon. It took forty days for the water to cover the earth in Noah's day. Forty days isn't very long on this earth. And I'm not relating that to a time on your calendar, but a time of God. Forty years, forty days.

In God's timing, you'll see a move of the Spirit of God upon this earth as Jesus is allowed to stand in the total center of our lives so that you can't get your eyes on angels, and you can't get your eyes on things or people. As you look, your eyes will be fixed on Him until He is the majesty, the royalty, the rulership of all; the Lord of our lives so completely that all we want to do is be in Him. When we get enough in Him that we can't see anything but His glory, then He merges into all of us and the world will see His glory within us.

It's as if this is a starting of a move that He is making. The clouds begin to come in and begin to cover the area. But His cloud of glory is getting ready to cover the whole earth. And it will come like the glory cloud that filled this room earlier tonight prior to His appearing.

That glory cloud is going to literally cover the earth until the rain of the Spirit comes in. But it's going to come in through people. It will be coming in as people yield to Him. Then the whole earth will be covered with His glory as the water covers the sea, as the clouds cover the sky. The whole earth will be filled with His glory, the sky will be filled with His glory, His majesty, His awesomeness.

We have experienced tonight, a room full of Jesus, a minority group of people. But He's got people like you across the world already. Each of these nuclei, each of these little rooms will burst forth and fill the space between these rooms until suddenly the gospel of Jesus Christ is spread over the whole earth through His people. People who will yield to Him so that He can be so in us that others will literally see His glory shining from us at all times.

Time is short, time is short. But time is ready, time is ready for those who are willing, for those who are willing to step into another world, a spirit world where the things of this earth matter not. Even if giant angels stood in mass, instantaneously they become dwarfed in His glory, in His presence, in His majesty, In His awesomeness.

And He is saying, "No longer are you going to be able to find satisfaction in the shallowness of an occasional dropping in on the Word of God." He is going to draw you in until you cannot put the Bible down. You'll discover that He will give you less need for sleep. You will be in Him for longer periods in the wee hours of the night, so you can be alone with Him in His Word. And then He will begin to become more in you.

And He is saying, "The time has arrived" to those who are willing to start spending hours in His Word and in meditation with Him. He will begin to fill each of you as a compacted explosive until you are so filled with Him that you'll actually explode into people around you.

It's going to come if you're willing to pay that price, if you're willing to wake up at night and simply spend time with Him.

Lay off of some of the other things that are using time. There are no priorities that are as important as spending time in Him, with Him, meditating with Him, talking with Him.

"Those who are willing, follow me, follow me into my glory cloud and you will see my glory!" saith the Lord God.

Hallelujah! Praise the Lord!

Following Charles' relating the vision and a message in tongues, Pastor Tom Tiemens interpreted the following Word from the Lord.

"Nothing shall stop My glory," says the Lord, "for it hath been spoken by My mouth. And that which I have spoken will be performed in the fullness of what I have designed it to be. So look to be enveloped with the Spirit

of My life," saith the Lord.

"Look to be enveloped of the One that I am and know that the glory, that I shall descend upon Him. That cloud upon this earth shall wrap around thee. And you shall walk in that glory and it shall come forth from you and it shall fill the earth as the waters cover the sea for the mouth of the Lord hath spoken it. And know that it is a glory that shall inhabit the entire peoples of the earth. And there shall not be one glory of one part of this earth and another glory to another, but it shall be a total glory that shall wrap around the very face of the earth.

"So, my people, walk in that envelope of My presence and see it come to pass," says the Lord.

"He who abides in Me, and I in him, bears much fruit; for without Me you can do nothing" (John 15:5 NKJV).

"And the glory which You gave Me I have given them, that they may be one just as We are one" (John 17:22 NKJV).

Chapter Two

A Vision

by Frances

Charles and I have a real problem where the things of God are concerned! We both want to give everything away that God gives to us.

Our personal stories are quite different. I was a *wild* sinner when I got saved! I was smoking five packages of cigarettes a day, drinking martinis like they were going out of style, was the life of every cocktail party because I knew more dirty jokes that anyone else, and couldn't open my mouth and say four words unless one of them was a swear word!

Then I met Jesus! And He turned my world around! I went to an altar a wild sinner, and because we're called to be saints, I rose up a saint of God! God placed in my heart an instant hate for evil. I looked at sin and it made me sick, so I turned and ran as fast as I could in the opposite direction. My life was completely transformed in that one single moment of time.

When I stood up from the altar, even though no one

counseled with me and no one prayed with me, I was an "instant" fanatic. In the twinkling of an eye, I had become a brand new creature in Christ! Somehow in a supernatural way which I do not understand to this day, God allowed me to instantly grasp and comprehend the principles of the Bible, even though I had never read it.

I understood there was no room for sin in the life of a Christian. I immediately understood that I had to die to self because Jesus had come to live inside of me. He was in my heart and I knew it! I had an instant revelation that I had to give away to everyone I met, what God had given to me. All of this had to be a supernatural revelation of the Holy Spirit, but whatever it was, I knew that holy living and total commitment were the only way to go.

I had stood there just moments before, totally oblivious to everything that surrounded me, only aware of the fact that I had made contact with a living God. I said, "God, I'll make a deal with you. I'll give you ALL of me, for all of YOU!" He accepted my offer and I gave away my total being to serve Him. Never again did the woman named Frances Gardner (my name at that time) live. It was a totally new creature who stood up with the knowledge branded on my heart that Jesus Christ, the Son of the Living God, was actually living His life in and through me.

That new creature took off like a rocket that day! My daughter and I got into the car together and I drove down the highway toward the shopping center where my printing company was located. I literally tried to "beat" Jesus Christ into the head of every person I met. Something had happened to me, and I had this zealous desire in me to give it away to everybody. I have often said, "Jesus Christ opened my mouth, and I haven't shut it since, and I don't intend to ever shut it where He's con-

cerned!"
I could not contain within myself the wonderful thing that happened to me. I was not a "silent" witness. There had been such a radical change in my life that I wanted every person with whom I came in contact to experience the same thing. There was a peace, a calm, a joy, a happiness, a zeal, and a fervor to share what had happened to me that could not be stopped! And I'm still the same way today!

Charles' story is a little different than mine. Charles was a "sweet" sinner whereas I had been a "nasty" sinner, but the end result would have been exactly the same.

Charles was a "good" man. He faithfully attended church, served on every committee and board in the church, was the treasurer of the church, sang in the choir, taught Sunday School, and did all the things a Christian was supposed to do. Yet, inside of him there was always a fear when lightning struck. He wasn't afraid of dying, he was just afraid of where he would go if he died. There was no security in his eternal destiny because at best, or at worst, whichever way you want to describe him, he was a carnal Christian. No BIG sins, no blatant sins, just little "secret" things about which he hoped God didn't know.

Faithful to his wife, outstanding in business, Charles would have never cheated anyone if his life had depended on it. He had an outstanding reputation as a Certified Public Accountant in Houston and to all outward appearances, he was a model Christian.

Inside of him, however, there was a hungering for something he had never been able to attain. He made trips to the altar time after time, "surrendering all," but returning exactly the same as when he went down.

Then one morning at a men's prayer breakfast where

men gathered for chatter, doughnuts and a short prayer session at an altar before going to work, Charles felt a supernatural drawing to God in a way he had never felt before. He knelt down and said, "God, take ALL of my life and make me spiritually what YOU want me to be!" and he recklessly threw himself at God as he turned loose of Charles Hunter. Result: he became an instant fanatic, too!

As I look back at the difference in our two lives, there is one remarkable similarity. Both of us, on the day we became an "instant" fanatic, said basically the same thing. We asked God to take ALL of our lives, and therein lies the secret. Neither of us had any desire to hold back anything for ourselves. Our only desire to live, breathe, eat and sleep was to serve Him.

"'If any of you wants to be my follower,' he told them, 'you must put aside your own pleasures and shoulder your cross, and follow me closely. If you insist on saving your life, you will lose it. Only those who throw away their lives for my sake and for the sake of the Good News will ever know what it means to really live'" (Mark 8:34,35 TLB).

Both of us have had an unmeasurable joy ever since then, and both of us stepped into a new strata of abundant living. We discovered the secret of knowing what it means to really live! We believe that if our spirit eyes had been opened to see what happened, we would have seen what looked like flames or tongues of fire appearing and settling on our heads just like on the day of Pentecost.

Peter loved Jesus with all his heart. He had given up his business to follow Him and sincerely would have been willing to give his life for Jesus, but he didn't. When his life was endangered by being identified with Jesus, Peter denied and even cursed Jesus. But when what looked like flames or tongues of fire appeared and settled on his head, the carnal Peter died to self, and Jesus was given total control of his life. Never again did Peter consider his own pleasure, but only wanted to lift up Jesus. He, too, became an instant fanatic!

The baptism with fire, which was prophesied by John when Jesus sent back the Holy Spirit, was given to burn the old carnal self-nature into dead ashes, so Jesus could be in absolute control of a life.

God brought the two of us together in a supernatural way, and after meeting while I was on a speaking tour in Houston, we were married eighty-eight days later without ever having a date with each other. Just eleven days before we were married, God spoke to me in Miami, Florida and without any human communication, spoke to Charles in Houston, Texas on the same day, telling us the exact minute, time and place we were to be married. He didn't ask us, He simply told us and we obeyed without any thought of questioning that God had spoken. We had totally released our lives to our God, and now He was telling us what He wanted us to do; we weren't asking Him to tell us.

We have just completed sixteen years of perfect marriage at the time of this writing, not because of Charles Hunter, not because of Frances Hunter, but because Jesus Christ is the center of our lives, our home and our marriage. (See MY LOVE AFFAIR WITH CHARLES.)

Both of us received exactly the same thing when we got saved, a burning fire within our very souls to share everything God had given to us with every person with whom we could make contact.

Not only did we want everyone saved and won to Jesus, but we wanted to teach them how to go out and share Jesus with others. We believed in our hearts that preaching the simple Gospel of salvation should be a normal part of a Christian's life. We held soul-winning classes all over the United States doing our best to give away what God had given to us...the burning zeal for souls that seemed to consume both of us.

Then came the great day when we received the baptism with the Holy Spirit in late 1971. We knew Jesus intended for us to do the same kind of miracles He did so people would believe in Him, but we had failed Him. Over 10,000 people came to us to be healed, and probably less than ten were healed. What was wrong?

Even though we had been taught against the doctrine of speaking in tongues, as soon as we yielded our hearts and were willing to speak in tongues,Jesus met us as the baptizer with the Holy Spirit.

Just as God had opened our hearts at the very beginning to the simplicity of the Gospel about salvation, He opened our understanding to the fact that when we were baptized with the Holy Spirit and spoke in tongues, we would be filled with the Spirit of God and would have the power that was missing to do miracles.

This magnified our desire to spread the Gospel, and we not only ministered the baptism to hundreds of thousands of hungry believers, but we began to give it away by teaching others how to minister the baptism successfully and naturally. We wrote the book THE TWO SIDES OF A COIN to let people know what a dynamic gift this was, but also to let them know it was the desire, the intention, and the commandment of Jesus that *all* would speak in tongues so they would be endued with God's power.

Shortly after we were married, we had a hunger in our hearts to start a little home Bible study. We were doing a limited amount of traveling at that time, but we were home often enough for Charles to take care of his CPA practice and for us to share our excitement and enthusiasm about what Jesus had done in our lives with other people. With no publicity, the "little" Bible study grew until we had one hundred and twenty-three people in our house one night. That's too many for anybody's house because we had them literally hanging from the chandeliers, so we decided to take our "little" Bible study to a nearby hotel. We outgrew the hotel in just a few months and decided to move to a local high school.

As we prayed and planned for our first night in a high school auditorium, we anticipated about one thousand people would be there. We realized that there was no way we could minister to that many people by ourselves. In our desire to give away everything that God had given us, we decided to teach our Board of Directors how to heal the sick so they could step off the stage with us and minister healing. We trained them so that we would all be ministering alike and all in one accord.

There is tremendous power in agreement. "One can put a thousand to flight, two can put ten thousand to flight."

Seven of us slowly walked down the stairs together in total agreement and as we did, the power of God exploded! God spoke words that are burned in our hearts: "THE DAY WILL COME WHEN YOU WILL STAND IN THE ASTRODOME WITH 120 HEALING TEAMS MINISTERING HEALING TO THE BODY OF CHRIST!" That was almost unbelievable to us.

Who are we to have a meeting in the Astrodome which seats more than 70,000 people?

But then, who are we to not believe God?

We tucked that vision away in our hearts and held it there for all these years. We never lost sight of the vision and would occasionally mention it to each other, but we waited until we again heard from God about this particular part of our ministry. Finally, in November of 1984, some eleven years later, God spoke through Russ Bixler, President of Channel 40 - WCTV, in Pittsburgh, Pennsylvania.

We were on his television program sharing the mighty and wondrous acts of God in the twentieth century when Russ turned to us and said, "I think you ought to hold a healing seminar on television to teach the people how to heal the sick!" Then he added, (and see how prophetic this was) "If you will come and do a healing seminar on TV, we'll assist you in scheduling a meeting to help with your expenses."

Our spirits immediately quickened to this, so when we came home we began to check our dates with Russ Bixler. Neither of us had a clearance in our spirits about the right dates. Suddenly, Russ said, "I believe God wants you to come to Pittsburgh for a healing seminar the week of July 4th and follow it with a big healing meeting at the Civic Arena on the 4th of July." Russ knew nothing about what God had told us years before, but the minute he said that, God immediately spoke to both Charles and me saying, "The first step to the Astrodome will be at the Pittsburgh Civic Arena on July 4th, 1985."

We literally exploded with excitement as we realized that God had not forgotten what He told us eleven years ago, but was starting to bring to pass that exciting vision. The thing that shocked us was that God chose such a big auditorium for our first healing "explosion"!

To the best of our knowledge this had never been done before. Never has a healing evangelist shared a meeting where one hundred and twenty teams, (person-

ally trained), would step out and minister healing to the body of Christ. We really began to pray. Could there possibly be two hundred and forty people with a vision of fulfilling the Great Commission as listed in Mark 16? Would we be able to encourage, attract, interest, exhort and convince enough people that the ordinary believer could heal the sick? Or would most of them say, "But I don't have the gift of healing!" Would there be enough who would understand that it is HIS POWER THROUGH YOU which causes healings?

All we knew was that we had to obey God. We also knew that we had heard God, and "if God be for us, who can be against us?" We immediately began to make arrangements for this "first-of-its-kind" meeting. There have been meetings where several well-known evangelists have ministered together, but never to our knowledge had it ever been done with "ordinary" believers who were *trained* to heal the sick.

God had specified the 4th of July, so in spite of extra charges because of the holiday, we rented the Pittsburgh Civic Arena. We shared this vision at the Pittsburgh Charismatic Conference which was held at Duquesne University on the mountain overlooking downtown Pittsburgh and the beautiful dome of the Civic Arena. We had the entire audience stand and point their hands toward the huge dome.

Our hearts thrilled at this sight. As we prayed for a mighty move of God in fulfillment of the vision He had given us years previously, giant angels suddenly appeared all around the dome with their feet standing on the "lip" and their bodies with outstretched arms reaching all the way to the top as though they were went to protect it until God began to manifest His glory, majesty and power on July 4th. Each time we went back to Pittsburgh to appear on TV and radio and minister in to Pittsburgh to appear on TV and radio and minister in area churches, the angels were always there. God had given us a supernatural sign that He was behind the meeting.

People began to realize that this was more than just another healing crusade. Soon letters began to come in from across the United States with such statements as:

"I want EVERY member of my congregation to participate in this great event!" from a pastor in Pittsburgh.

From California came this statement, "Praise God for airplanes - we can fly there for this one great day and be back in time for work the next. Wouldn't miss it for anything."

From Dallas, Texas: "Our church is saving their money so we can fly to Pittsburgh to participate in this great event."

From a Houston, Texas pastor: "That's where I'm going to celebrate the 4th of July!"

From Erie, Pennsylvania, "We'll be there with a busload. We don't want to miss what God is doing!"

From Quincy, Illinois, "We're going to be there to worship and praise, usher, sell books or do whatever is necessary.

A Houston pastor said, "This really has stirred my spirit. I believe it will be the greatest thing ever done by the body of Christ. I'm going to see if our congregation can charter a plane and attend. We don't want to miss it!"

From Ramseur, N.C. came the message, "We are coming a week early with our soul-winning teams to work on Pittsburgh streets. We are trying to get a whole bus from here."

Charles spoke prophetically: "As we look at the end generation and our responsibility to Jesus to accomplish the maximum in the short time we have left before His coming, we look with an overview of what is the most important work in the body of Christ, and how do we accomplish it? There isn't much time left, so what we must do, we must do quickly.

"Since over half of the world has never heard the name of Jesus, and a large percentage of those who have heard do not really know Him personally, we see the Great Commission as the central function of the body of Christ from now until the return of Jesus. That is what we must do NOW...and do it quickly.

"The part of the Great Commission so overlooked and ignored is the prophecy and command that EVERY BELIEVER would preach the gospel (win people to Jesus and make them into disciples who will win people to Jesus), and EVERY BELIEVER would do this with supernatural power in miracles, signs and wonders.

"We believe this one meeting will trigger a release in the hearts of EVERY BELIEVER that each one is to do miracles as a sign to the unbelievers, a supernatural sign which will cause them to see Jesus alive today, doing His work through ordinary, everyday, miracle-working BELIEVERS."

Chapter Three

People Healing People

During this twentieth century, God has raised up many giant healing evangelists to do His mighty acts. In our relatively short span of miracle ministry since 1972, we have seen an ever-increasing acceleration of healings. In the beginning we would see an occasional miracle healing in our services. Then came the night when God dropped us into a healing ministry.*

We began to see several healed at every meeting. Miracles continued to increase until we were seeing perhaps more than ten percent of those coming for healing receive every night!

Then one hot summer night in Michigan we saw another dramatic increase in results. Ushers came to us at the end of the service saying it seemed as if everyone was healed. In our own hearts we felt that at least eighty percent of those who came for healing received immediate visible miracles. Others wrote later that they

*As told in our book SINCE JESUS PASSED BY.

were healed of sicknesses such as heart problems and diabetes as well as other diseases in which healings are not discernable without a doctor's examination.

It has been awesome and overwhelming to us to go down a healing line and see almost everyone healed night after night. It is no longer a "hit and miss" and "hope for healing," but it is approaching the likes of the ministry of Jesus when every person was healed. But, isn't that what Jesus said would happen? You believers, He said, will do the works He did while on earth, and even greater works.

It really hasn't surprised us as much as astounded us to see what Jesus is doing through ordinary people. It really shouldn't surprise any of us believers, when we all know by the Spirit that this is the closing generation of this age before the return of Jesus.

Jesus wrote to us in the Great Commission just before He left this earth 2,000 years ago, that EVERY BELIEVER would preach the gospel, cast out devils, speak in tongues (the baptism with the Holy Spirit and enduing of power), handle snakes (our enemies and the devil) and his poisons would not harm us, and we believers ALL would lay hands on the sick and they would be healed. This has been done only by a very few people who seemingly were a special chosen person or persons to do miracles. We speak of the great healing ministries of those few as though they were something unusual and very special.

But that isn't what Jesus said would happen. He simply said that ALL BELIEVERS would do these works and miracles so that people would believe in Him and would thereby receive eternal life.

God began teaching us various ways to apply His power with the authority vested in us by Jesus as believers. Besides seeing mighty signs and wonders worked through our hands, we began to give every secret God revealed to us to everyone who would listen and believe.

Just as salvation was made simple to us, and we could teach others to lead people to Jesus, the baptism with the Holy Spirit was made simple to us, and we could teach others how to effectively minister this great gift to others, we discovered that the supernatural could be taught.

We held seminars around the world, teaching people how to heal the sick, to operate in the gifts of the Holy Spirit, and how to do other supernatural things. We realized that the Holy Spirit had taught us each of the supernatural things we were doing by His power, and we very simply taught others what He had taught us. We stumbled and failed many times, but we persisted in learning and teaching until we now are seeing giant footsteps in the body of Christ Jesus by ordinary believers.

We conducted a Bible School primarily to teach the simplicity of the Gospel, and to teach the students HOW TO DO WHAT JESUS SAID TO DO AND WHAT HE DID WHILE ON EARTH.

We purchased television equipment and video taped all of these teachings. If God had no other purpose in the Bible School and television than to record the original twelve hours on HOW TO HEAL THE SICK, the six hours on the HOLY SPIRIT and the six hours on HOW TO DEVELOP THE GIFTS OF THE SPIRIT, it would have been worth the three years we devoted to that ministry. God was not only preparing us for the special work with believers for which He had called us, but He was preparing the tools with which we could teach multitudes around the world HOW TO HEAL THE SICK and HOW TO OPERATE IN THE VALUABLE GIFTS OF

THE HOLY SPIRIT!

There was a degree of success as people watched the video and studied our book TO HEAL THE SICK, but there were relatively few who really got the vision that ALL BELIEVERS should be daily doing all the work Jesus and the disciples and apostles did while they began the church age.

Then came PITTSBURGH with the FIRST Healing Explosion in the history of the world! God's time had arrived when this ministry by ALL believers would spread rapidly around the world!

What is a Healing Explosion?

That is the name which seemed to best describe what God was opening up as the first giant step toward the fulfillment of the vision He had spoken into our hearts about the 120 healing teams ministering as a unified force in the Astrodome. We felt in our spirits that a new beginning of the end-generation ministry was exploding to usher in the great harvest of souls and the rapture of the Church!

This first Healing Explosion which was to be held in Pittsburgh would be the first time when the so-called "healing evangelist" would turn the miracle work over to a host of ordinary believers who had been trained to heal the sick. To our knowledge this had never been done before. It would be a miracle service of the people, by the people and for the people with PEOPLE HEALING PEOPLE!

We immediately sent out a request for prayer warriors. "Again I say unto you, That if two of you shall agree on earth as touching any thing that they shall ask, it shall be done for them of my Father which is in heaven. For where two or three are gathered together in my name, there am I in the midst of them" (Matthew

18:19,20 KJV).

We needed people to PRAY that the hearts of thousands of believers would be quickened to the eternal importance of this particular "first-of-its-kind" meeting. We asked them to PRAY that thousands would want to be there to be a living part of this end-time demonstration of the potential within each member of the body of Christ to actually do the work of Jesus using the same power with which He did His work while He was on earth.

We asked prayer warriors to PRAY that hundreds and hundreds would want to be workers as ushers, reporters, helpers, healing teams and other multitudes of jobs to be done. We asked those prayer partners to PRAY that God would alert thousands who needed salvation and the baptism with the Holy Spirit, those who needed healing and deliverance, or a purpose in their lives for Jesus, to make plans to be there.

We asked them to pray for the finances of the meeting, because we were going to spend more money than we had ever spent for one meeting in all of our ministry. We asked God for wisdom, strength and spiritual power so that we could properly lead the people in this very important work for Jesus. We asked the prayer warriors to PRAY that God would raise up bus captains as well as those who would ride the buses into Pittsburgh. Our list of prayer requests were taken to the very throneroom of God by outstanding prayer warriors. God heard and answered!

We had one of our newspapers ready for the press when God spoke to us and we quickly inserted a little ad in it which mentioned the Healing Explosion. The very day the first tabloid was delivered, I received a telephone call from a Pittsburgh businessman named Joe Horst,

"What can I do to help? My spirit leaped within me when I saw the news of the Healing Explosion! I want to help!"

I said, "What can you do?"

He replied, "What do you need done?"

I replied, "Everything! What do you do for a living?"

He said, "I'm a public relations man!!"

I said, "Great! You can be the coordinator." He immediately accepted!

"It shall come to pass That before they call, I will answer; And while they are still speaking, I will hear" (Isaiah 65:24 NKJV). Before we had even realized that we needed a local coordinator for the meeting, God had raised up such a man and sent him to us. If it had not been for Joe's untiring efforts, we could never have accomplished all that was done in preparation for that meeting. How we praise God that He knows which man to touch and speak to for such a job as this!

We advertised and talked about what God had told us all over the United States. The message went to foreign countries, and three of them had representatives at the Pittsburgh Healing Explosion.

As the plan began to formulate, we decided we would require everyone who wanted to be on the healing teams to view the twelve hours of video on HOW TO HEAL THE SICK or to listen to the same twelve hours of audio tapes AND to study the book, TO HEAL THE SICK. Then we would have the teams come to Pittsburgh three days early to go through live training where we could up-date the teachings with new revelations God had taught us, to review the teachings and reinforce them in their hearts and minds, and to inspire them to walk into the arena with giant faith to do all the works Jesus would do if He were there in person. Praise God, He was there personally doing His work through more than 1,000 believers by the power of God's Holy Spirit.

We were further delighted when doctors and chiropractors joined us on a panel to explain how various illnesses and injuries affected the body and what to do by God's power to get the body divinely healed. What an awesome teaching this brought about! We both received tremendous insights into ways to get more and more people healed. It seemed that understanding healings was made clear and simple to us...and to the "baby" healing teams who would be doing the actual healing the third day of training.

The final day seemed to rush upon all of us and the time came when over 1,000 newly trained "ordinary believers" would be responsible for an audience of 11,000 people who came expecting this new way to work for them.

Would they be hesitant to go to people with little or no healing experience, to those who possibly never ministered healings before? Would they have wrong attitudes when they could not come directly to Charles and Frances, the healing evangelists that God uses so mightily in getting people healed?

We had a few who tried to reach us, but almost everyone accepted this new concept of ministering personally and individually to large masses of people. It would have been impossible for the two of us to lay hands on more than perhaps a thousand or fifteen hundred. We often minister for two and three hours or even longer to touch our normal size audiences.

But God has a simple but effective plan through these Healing Explosions to touch the whole world with His message of salvation, the baptism with the Holy Spirit and fire, and His healing touch.

God's end-generation ministry of people healing people had finally dramatically come about in Pittsburgh at this first historical Healing Explosion! The ordinary people with such a small amount of training actually did do mighty acts for God. They amazingly did more than we had ever dreamed or imagined possible. Jesus is still alive in His people, and He will accomplish the preparation of the body of Christ for His triumphant return.

Simply said, Jesus told us two thousand years ago, put it in writing and spoke words that traveled through time to reach our hearts and ears in this twentieth century, that we ALL would be doing just what He demonstrated in this first overwhelmingly amazing ministry of ordinary believers doing miracles to glorify the Father in the Son Jesus!

The day of "people healing people" was born July 4, 1985!

"On July 4, 1776, in the city of Philadelphia, Pa. there was signed one of America's greatest historic documents, the Declaration of Independence. We celebrate this day in many ways. But usually, ending the day with fireworks.

On July 4, 1985, in the city of Pittsburgh, over 200 years later in another city in Pennsylvania, God gave the independence He wants His people to have.

"Fireworks? The best I've ever seen!"

It was like water slowly draining down a funnel to a strainer where the fire of God's Holy Spirit boiled the water until it was made clean and the impurities were strained out."

And it brought unity...

"Behold, how good and how pleasant it is For brethren to dwell together in unity" (Psalms 133:1 NKJV).

We have never experienced such unity in the Body of Christ as we saw in Pittsburgh as believers from many churches and groups worked together to bring 11,000 people to the Pittsburgh Civic Arena to see the glory of God displayed!

When Russ Bixler of WCTV, Channel 40, in Pittsburgh said that God had spoken to him about having five nights of healing teaching on TV so his listeners could learn how to heal the sick, to be followed by the meeting at the Civic Arena, we immediatley began working with the leaders and workers in the Pittsburgh area to make the giant meeting the success it was for Jesus to be so mightily exalted.

Russ and Norma Bixler opened their hearts and TV ministry and continued week after week to let people know about the meeting, to excite them about coming and to build their faith for the final tremendous results of the hundreds and even thousands to be healed and lives changed.

Many people were healed as we worked with Russ and Norma teaching their TV audiences HOW TO HEAL THE SICK. The anointing was tremendous as we shared together and prepared the people for the great explosion. One lady even came to the studio to "show off" the filling God put in a tooth while she was watching the teaching. People who came to the studio to watch the program "live" were also healed and touched by the power of God.

God had been working in many ways and through many people in the Pittsburgh area to bring a mighty move of the Spirit. One prophecy which appears significant was given by Reverend John Garlington at the Pittsburgh Charismatic Conference in 1983, and was actually an announcement of what would happen at the July 4th Healing Explosion:

"The Lord brought something back to me. Some years ago I saw a vision, standing in Pittsburgh, and I just believe that this is the time God is going to release that thing. I stood some place praying and saw sheep streaming down out of the hills, and shepherds with them. God is going to move upon shepherds, pastors, throughout this area again and they are going to flow again in the purpose of God. The sheep will all be gathered. God is going to move in local churches to knit the hearts of pastors together. They are going to stand as one, for as they stand as one, that will release the glory and power of God in areas pushing back principalities and powers, releasing God's presence and power."

At a pastors' and workers' breakfast, many different denominations were represented including Assembly of God, Baptist, Catholic, Mennonite, Brethren, Presbyterian, Episcopalian, Lutheran, Church of God Pentecostal, Methodist, Word of Faith, plus many others. The spirit of unity was beautiful to watch and see the cooperation of all those attending.

Chapter Four

The Fulfillment of the Vision Begins

"From the moment Charles and Frances appeared at the end of the great arena, the anointing of God covered and smothered the Pittsburgh Civic Arena. As they made their way toward the stage, it was as if the bride of Christ was walking down the aisle to meet Jesus. Truly this meeting was the most anointed one I have ever attended in all of my life. I wept almost from beginning to end because the presence of God was so strong." Betty Tapscott, Chairman of the Board, Hunter Ministries, and author of "Inner Healing Through Healing of Memories", "Set Free", "Fruit of the Spirit" and other books.

We could not help but feel the same way once we stepped up onto the stage. The Victory Processional March started with anointed children and singers from the Living Word Christian Outreach Center in Lincoln, Nebraska. They had come to share their love of God and anointing with others attending the first Healing Explosion. As they began to sing "WE PROCLAIM THE NAME OF THE LORD," thousands began to weep.

The impact it had on our spirits was that this truly was the beginning of the end-time ministry of the *believers* to do the works of Jesus and even greater things than He did while on earth. As the children marched triumphantly with banners declaring the names of God and Jesus, it was as though we were all in one accord proclaiming not only the mighty name of the Lord, but the beginning of a new ministry of Jesus!

As we watched a video of what was shown on TV the next day, we again wept because of the powerful anointing on this meeting! It was a moment to be savored and treasured forever.

At the conclusion of the march, Bob and Joan Barker (our children) and their eight-year-old daughter, Charity, led in the pledge of allegiance to the flag and dramatically ended it with "in Jesus' name"!

We seemed to enter the very throne room of God as 11,000 expectant worshippers lifted their hands and voices in a unified burst of adoration and praise of our Master! Healings were reported to have occurred during this time of powerful praise and worship.

Almost at the very beginning of the service we led the entire audience in a prayer for salvation. Thousands raised their hands at this time. However one of the biggest surprises of the entire meeting came when over 5,000 stood to receive the baptism with the Holy Spirit! God's people were hungry for the power of God in their lives...and they were filled!

When that exciting moment came for the healing teams to begin to operate, there was a tremendous air of expectancy and the stands literally seemed to empty as believers surged forward to have hands laid upon them. Many individuals stated it looked like an army was attacking the devil!

We had asked the healing teams to write down the healings that took place, but they got so excited about seeing so many people healed by the power of God, they forgot all about keeping records. They just kept laying hands on more and more people so God's supernatural healing power could flow through them. It was not until the Victory Breakfast the next morning that we heard these overwhelmed, excited believers share the mighty miracles which occurred through their hands on this awesome "first night"!

By seven o'clock that night, most of the crowd had gone home, and just a few of the healing teams remained. Those in charge of removing all of our belongings from the arena were hard at work when a man came in pushing a woman in a wheelchair. They had mistakenly arrived at 7 p.m. instead of 2 p.m. One of the healing teams that remained ministered salvation to her first and then healing. Praise God! No one is ever too late for God's healing power!

As we left the arena that night, we took one last look to see and remember the mighty things God had done. Left strewn around the massive auditorium, we saw hearing aids, crutches, leg braces, foot braces, tooth braces and many other visible but silent signs that God's power had been there.

Pittsburgh now is but fond history - the birth of a new era in the lives of the turned-on Christians who were touched that day.

Exciting prophecies came forth upon several occasions, one of which followed some tremendous worship (when everyone was lost in the Spirit, hungering to do all that God had called us to do) and was delivered by Pastor Tom Tiemens of Fresno, California at one of the training sessions prior to the meeting. We all stood in awe as God revealed His plans for each and every one of us.

"Now the Lord is mighty in song, yea, even the Lord your God has rejoiced over singing this day. The Lord is mighty in battle, the Lord is mighty in song. The Lord has come by His Spirit, and yea, He has graced each and every one and you shall move as a mighty army, a mighty army, saith the Lord. Great shall be the destruction of the enemy's camp, saith the Lord. Great shall be his destruction, for we are living in those days prophesied by the prophets of old. Yea, these are the last days, saith the Lord, and the enemy shall not withstand my people. Yea, my people are rising. They are standing as they have never stood before and the work that I shall do in them shall be a great work.

"Things that took great lengths of time shall not take great lengths of time, but I shall accelerate my activities. I shall accelerate growth in the lives of my people and my people shall grow quickly for the time of the Lord, the day of the Lord is at hand and there is a work that must be done in this land, saith the Lord, so rejoice in the Lord that speaks to you now, for surely your God shall equip you with a supernatural plow. You'll put that into the ground and you'll run, saith the Lord, and the enemy's lands shall be open before you and you shall lay demons on this side, and demons on that side. Yea, you shall finish the course that I have set before you, and great shall be the rejoicing of the Lord in this hour and in this day, saith the Lord.

"There have been days, yes, and even weeks, and even years of frustration and disappointment. You may think that you're here to turn the captivity of others, and

*yes, that shall happen, but I want you to know that I have
brought you to this place to turn YOUR captivity this
day, says the Lord. Your captivity shall be turned, saith
the Lord, and when you leave this place you shall go forth
as kindling and where you go revival shall take place,
and shall not be quenched!*

*"Be warned, saith the Lord. Be warned, for the
enemy shall come. He'll try to contest the thing that I
shall do in your life this week, saith the Lord, but if you'll
stand contending for the faith that I have delivered to
you, yea, the enemy shall not succeed in his plans against
you and revival shall come and you shall be the instru-
ment that I shall use to change churches, to change
neighborhoods, to change communities, to change cities,
to change nations, saith the Lord.*

*"You are part of this mighty army, and my camp is
very great. Did I not say these things? Did I not say that
my glory would fill the earth? Did I not say these things of
the latter days, of the end-time days? This is the hour,
these are the latter days, and these are the end-times and
I have an army that I'm going to reveal at this time. The
enemy has never seen the likes of this army.*

*"The Army of God is not limited to this nation; the
Army of God is within every nation and every kindred
and every tongue. I'm going to show the enemy that he
cannot mess with me in these last days and you, the
people of God, shall prove me, saith the Lord!"*

There were several words from the Lord which came
out on that great day, and one that excited us tremendously was a very short one but one which brought into
focus the purpose for the July 4th Healing Explosion.

God spoke through prophecy:

*"Hunter Ministries and the Healing Explosions will
be used by the Lord to birth other ministries as the saints*

do minister. I am using the Spiritual Awakening training to insure enough ministries to handle the revival which has begun to sweep the United States via Pittsburgh, Lakeland, Denver and other places."

Somewhere in the neighborhood of 1,000 new ministries were birthed on July 4th, 1985 at the Civic Arena in Pittsburgh, Pa. One pastor gave the members of the healing teams half of the next Sunday morning service for testimonies and that evening had a "mini" healing explosion. Reports say that nearly 100% of the people who came for healings received exactly what they came for.

God spoke through a vision:

A radio engineer said he was whisked away in the Spirit for just a few moments. During this period he saw Jesus dancing in the Spirit. A thought entered his mind, "That's not very religious..." and then another thought came..."But it's very scriptural."

Read Luke 10:19-20. In the next verse it says, "Jesus rejoiced in the Spirit..." In the original Hebrew this means "twirled around with reckless abandon!" Jesus was rejoicing over the fact that He was seeing the Great Commission being fulfilled in the twentieth century in Pittsburgh on July 4th!

"'The glory of this latter temple shall be greater that the former,' says the Lord of hosts. 'And in this place I will give peace,' says the Lord of hosts" (Haggai 2:9 NKJV).

To say it was an "EXPLOSION" is like saying TNT is a firecracker.

Prophecy given by Pastor Larry DiAngi of Erie, Pennsylvania:

"Yea, my son and my daughter, I have found thee a faithful couple. Yea, I have found thee a couple that shall see My glory. Yea, and shall not take it unto thyself, yea

but shall pass it quickly unto Me. Yea, and because thou hast allowed My Spirit to move and thou hast been content to make Me the star, yea and thou hast not seen thyselves as stars, but thou hast said, 'Jesus, thou art the Star in our lives and yea, even in our ministry.'

I say unto thee this night that this day marks a new day, saith the Lord, in thy lives. Yea, even in thy marriage and even in thy ministry thou shalt see a breaking forth on every side, saith the Lord. Yea, in all the healings and all the greatness and all the glory and all the miracles that thou hast seen these last fifteen years, I say from this night forward; yea, and even a year from this night in the next three hundred and sixty-five days thou shalt see more miracles than thou hast seen in the last fifteen years, saith God.

"For I even have had thee in preparation, saith the Lord; yea, I have been preparing thee and I have been watching thee. I have been watching thee. I have been watching to see if thou wouldst take unto thyselves that which belongeth to Me. Yea, but I have seen thee over and over and over and over say, 'Lord, it is not ours; We give it unto Thee.' Yea, and I have found thee and I have seen that I can trust thee. Yea, begin to see a greater enlarging, saith the Lord. For again, I would say unto thee in the next year, thou shalt see greater than thou hast seen in the last fifteen, saith God."

Another word from the Lord came through Pastor Tim O'Leary of Jackson, Mississippi, and it said,

"For the Spirit of the Lord would say this day that this day and time and this hour has been recorded in the calendar of heaven since the beginning of time. Think it not strange that this day is the day of your independence. For it is the day also that ye celebrate your independence in the Kingdom of God. This day has been marked by the

Spirit that you may know that this is a new era. For it is written in the scriptures that the latter days shall be greater than the former days, and so it shall be that you shall have the double portion, for it is no accident that ye have chosen the 240 and yea even more to be sent out, for it is twice as many as the day of Pentecost in the early days.

"For it shall be in this day that the Spirit of God is going to be manifested and the glory of the Lord will be revealed in a double portion through many. This is not the day of the ministry gift but the day of the believer, for this decade shall be known as the decade of the supernatural. The ministry gifts have been perfected and they have been perfecting the saints for this time that the believer may go forth and perform the great commission which was given you by Christ the Lord, the head of the church.

"And know that this is no strange hour for peculiar things to take place in the Spirit for there shall come anointings that men have not yet seen or experienced. And this is the day of group ministry. The day of the one-man ministry has come to an end. For have you not read in the scriptures, saith the Lord, that in the days of Samuel, there were the sons of the prophets that ministered and traveled together. And have you not read when Agabus, the prophet, in the book of Acts came down with a group from Jerusalem" (Acts 11:27-28).

"So it shall be, even as Jesus sent them out two by two and three by three that YOU shall be called of God. Many even here this day shall be touched before you leave with the anointing power to heal. And you shall go forth in groups and even on platforms of many arenas in these United States. You shall begin to behold ministry gifts. And they shall minister together: The apostle with

the prophet; the prophet with the evangelist; the evangelist with the teacher; the teacher with the pastor. And there shall be many in diverse kinds of operations and many groups ministering. This shall come about that it will be as prophesied that these latter days shall be greater than the former days...

"You shall see everything in this generation. The Spirit of the Lord shall brood upon children. And even the younger ones shall rise up with healing in their hands. And they shall move out within schools and within the neighborhoods. And yes, among the relatives and they shall have a healing touch that will completely astound the wise of this world.

"For the Spirit of the Lord is pouring Himself out in this last day. And mark it by the Spirit - this is the last day. This is the last generation. And the glory of God is going to be manifested. The secret of His power, the secret of the power of healing which you shall have exhibited and demonstrated before your eyes this day in various ways...

"So stand tall and stand firm this day, for this area has been marked by God to be a pioneer work to begin and work across this nation. And you shall see meetings like this abound from here on out as people come together from all faiths, all denominations, and they shall receive from the Spirit of God and barriers shall be broken."

These messages were not only for those in Pittsburgh, but for *all* believers. It is to *you* and to *us*, in these days. We believe that the first prophecy with the comments about the increase in healings applies to our ministry in particular and to those to whom we have passed it on! That means *YOU!*

As you meditate on the word from the Lord through

Tim O'Leary's message, visualize in your spirit that you are a part of that great group ministry mentioned. Listen as God said the day of the one-man ministry is over. How exciting it is to be a part of this end-time ministry which says that every believer will lay hands on the sick, cast out devils, speak with new tongues and preach the gospel.

It is hard for the finite mind to absorb all that God has for the body of Christ, and all that He yearns to do and will do through them.

We had seated the members of the healing teams in chairs around the floor of the arena, and before we released them to lay hands on the sick, we anointed them and passed on to them all of the gifts of the Spirit in which we operate.

One man wrote: "I would like to convey that the healing teams around the circle of the arena were like the 'hem of Christ's garment'. When people came in contact with the team, they were healed. The teams represented the hem of His garment that others saw in the vision of Christ above us in the dome of the Civic arena."

The fulfillment of the vision begins as the birth of a new age!

Chapter Five

Who Heals the Sick...

*A Teaching on the Hunters' Book,
To Heal the Sick*

by Russ Bixler

*President of Cornerstone TeleVision, Inc. WCTV-TV,
Channel 40, Pittsburgh, and WKBS-TV, Channel 47, Al-
toona, Pa., B.A., M.A., M. Div. plus graduate work. Ordained minister, Church of the Brethren.*

Charles and Frances Hunter have written a very interesting book, TO HEAL THE SICK. More than interesting, it is controversial! To summarize their thesis,
Jesus did not instruct believers to "pray" that God would
heal the sick; rather, He said, "...those who believe...will
lay hands on the sick, and they will recover" (Mark
16:17,18). This article is a biblical exposition of their
teaching on the subject of healing.

The book is quite scriptural, but the Hunters do not
always give the scriptural basis for their teachings and
illustrations. Actually, their real-life illustrations remind us of the biblical pattern of storytelling. The Bible

is not self-consciously a book of theology; rather, it is largely a recounting of the mighty acts of God. In the New Testament God normally uses people to accomplish these mighty acts. First, Jesus of Nazareth performs miracles, healings and deliverances from evil spirits. Second, His disciples perform miracles, healings and deliverances. The supernatural occurrences (1) glorify God, (2) strengthen the church, and (3) provide a dynamic for evangelization.

In the Old Testament the Holy Spirit fell only upon certain favored, sovereignly chosen persons. We find in the New Testament however that the Holy Spirit is available to all believers in Jesus Christ. Therefore, *any Christian* can be empowered to perform miracles, healings and deliverances, even as described in Acts.

Most of the healings recorded in the four Gospels were accomplished by Jesus of Nazareth. But in the midst of His ministry He sent out His followers to do the same - first the twelve, and then seventy others. His instruction? "Heal the sick, raise the dead, cleanse lepers, cast out demons" (Matthew 10:8). "And they departed and went through the villages, preaching the gospel and healing everywhere" (Luke 9:6). Never do we find in the Gospels any suggestion that the disciples prayed that God would heal; they simply healed the sick. They were thrilled to discover that demons had to leave at the mention of Jesus' name.

The Acts of the Apostles is a very appropriately titled book, because it is full of just such acts. I was taught in seminary that the book should have been called "The Acts of the Holy Spirit", but I have long since realized that the anonymous titler was quite correct in the first place. The book does indeed describe the acts of the apostles; they did the miracles attested; the scripture says so!

The Bible contains not one recorded incident of the early Christians having prayed for the sick in the sense of asking God to heal them. The first generation church simply healed the sick. The healings begin with the narrative in Acts 3 where Peter, accompanied by John, spoke to the crippled man, "I have no silver and gold, but I give you what I have; in the name of Jesus Christ of Nazareth, walk." Peter merely issued the command in Jesus' name. This incident establishes the subsequent pattern for the miracles and healings in the early church.

Many additional instances are recorded of the early Christians having accomplished miracles and healings, even dispensed punishment, through the spoken word and in the name of Jesus. Not one story suggests that these bold disciples of the Lord ever prayed for healing: they simply and obediently healed. Note each of the many relevant scriptures: Acts 4:30; 5:9-10; 6:8; 8:13,17; 9:17,34,40; 13:11; 14:3,10; 15:12; 16:18; 19:6,11-12; 20:10; 28:8-9. Every one of these scriptures is either a direct testimony or a reference to the commands of the early Christians as they performed the miraculous.

Other New Testament allusions to the overall subject illustrate the fact that early Christians never prayed for miracles, but rather spoke them into existence: Romans 15:18-19; II Corinthians 10:5-6; 12:12; 13:10; I Peter 4:10; even the two witnesses of Revelations 11:4-6, whoever they are, are to accomplish miracles through their spoken words.

Some have protested that the basic scripture used by Charles and Frances Hunter is from a later addition to Chapter 16 of the Gospel accoding to Mark, a total of 12 verses, 9 through 20. It is true that these final verses of Mark are not in several of the most ancient Greek manuscripts of the New Testament. Mark himself may not have written them; perhaps this portion was added by a later scribe. Such a possibility, however, does not lessen the value of these verses, for even the last chapter of the Gospel according to John seems to have been added by a subsequent editor.

Even if the final verses of Mark had been written at a later date, that would add *increased* meaning and purpose, since a later writer, if he existed, was merely recording what he had already seen and experienced. He would have been describing those miracles that the early Christians had regularly been accomplishing, including "they will lay their hands on the sick, and they will recover." Obviously such miracles had been occurring and were still occurring with great regularity and this alleged later scribe would simply have been reporting - with excitement - what had been going on. Therefore these final twelve verses would be removed from the realm of mere prophecy and placed in the realm of actual events.

The closing verse of the Gospel according to Mark is the summary statement of how miracles operate in Christian practice: "And they went forth and preached everywhere, while the Lord worked with them and confirmed the message by the signs that attended it. Amen." The Lord "works with" His people; and as they preach the Word and command healing and deliverance, the power of the Lord is always present to fulfill believers' commands. Miracles are thus the normative accompaniment of any Spirit-filled Christian's witnessing.

Some doubters refer to the anointing ordinance, James 5:14-18, declaring that we should "pray" for the sick. James uses the word "pray" or "prayer" six times in that passage. However, James means more—much more

— by that word than we modern Americans. He refers to Elijah's praying that it not rain and later praying that it rain once again. But, looking back to I Kings 17:1 and 18:41-45, we find that Elijah didn't "ask" God to withhold the rain; he *commanded* that it not rain. Elijah's subsequent word to commence the rain after a prolonged drought is also clearly implied. Therefore James, in trying to be faithful to the original story, must have meant more than merely "ask" when he used the word "pray".

The one other New Testament reference to the anointing for healing is found in Mark 6:13, "And they cast out many demons, and anointed with oil many that were sick and healed them." Again, there are no requests made of God; but rather, the disciples "healed them", the oil symbolizing the Holy Spirit who provides the power.

One might protest further that Jesus instructed His disciples, "If you ask anything in my name, I will do it" (John 14:14). Again, we find a richer intent in the word "ask". The original Greek word often means to "ask for", or "demand", as it does in I Corinthians 1:22, "...Jews demand signs..."

We could illustrate the point by imagining that you are requesting of a stranger on the street, "please give me a hundred dollars." Not much chance of success! Then imagine your taking your savings deposit book to a bank teller — even a stranger — and speaking the very same words. Of course, this second response would be different. The bank teller would respond quickly with the money. The usage in John 14:14 has the latter intent; the miracles are already on deposit through the blood of Jesus Christ, and now you may "ask" for them.

I first heard a presentation similar to the Hunters' about 10 years ago while I was ministering at a retreat with Herbert Mjorud, the Lutheran evangelist from Minneapolis. I had to acknowledge that what Herbert was saying was scriptural, but something within me was causing me to want to ignore it in actual practice. I realize now that I was being deterred by a false modesty. After all, who was I to say that I could heal? Only God heals! And so I resisted this teaching for a period.

Perhaps a false modesty prevents us all from feeling we can command the Holy Spirit's actions; yet that is exactly what the early Christians did, and our response is to be, like theirs, obedient. Our refusal to command healing in the name of Jesus is plain disobedience, not humility! Satan uses our false modesty to deter the church from doing the full work of God.

There are clear indications in the scriptures that Jesus has already accomplished all that the Father sent Him to do: "It is finished!" He cries from the cross. Then on Pentecost, He gave us the Holy Spirit so we could accomplish our mission until He returns. Paul states in Colossians 1:24 that "in my flesh I complete what is lacking in Christ's afflictions for the sake of His body, that is, the Church."

We do have a commission to fulfill in the name of Jesus. This is further confirmed by Luke's opening statement in the Book of Acts: "In the first book, O Theophilus, I have dealt with all that Jesus began to do and teach.." Jesus began to do and teach many things. But by filling each of us with His Spirit, He is enabling all of us together to accomplish lots more. So He sent the Spirit of God by whose power we can *all* fulfill His enormous commandments. Without that power we can barely make a dent in the awesome tasks. When we know His will, we are to *do* it! Only false modesty causes us to hesitate to command the Power Who has been placed within us.

We might imagine Moses standing on the shore, looking back and seeing the Egyptian army, and looking ahead seeing the Red Sea. He must have complained to God for "...the Lord said to Moses, 'Why do you cry to me? Tell the people of Israel to go forward. Lift up your rod, and stretch out your hand over the sea and divide it, that the people of Israel may go on dry ground through the sea'" (Exodus 14:15,16).

Moses must have thought immediately, "Who, me?" Yet God's directive is exactly what happened after Moses obeyed. As Moses lifted up his rod and demanded that the sea divide, a strong east wind came up, and by daybreak the bottom of the Red Sea was exposed. This power that we see in the command of Moses is now given to *every* believer who has been filled with the Holy Spirit. Through Jesus Christ, God has restored to us the dominion that Adam relinquished so many centuries ago. We have this authority, we have this dominion and we have His instruction to heal, but very few Christians have the maturity, the courage and the obedience to stir up the Power dwelling within them.

God seems to have a great trust in His people. I am amazed that He would entrust me with His Holy Spirit. I wouldn't trust myself.

Apparently, God wants some sign of my obedience, and therefore, He has asked that I give him my voice. We know from the letter of James that the tongue is like the rudder of a ship. Where it says I will go, I go. What it says I will do, I do. So God asks me to give over control of my tongue to Him, and He puts a language on it that I do not understand. To the natural man this is foolishness, as Paul says in I Corinthians 2, but this just may be God's means of sorting out the obedient from the stubborn. He apparently has decided that those who are too proud to give their voices to the Spirit of God cannot have the Power; but to those who are humble enough to do so, God will entrust His Power. I remain utterly amazed at God's confidence in us Christians — we who are imperfect even at our best and disgusting at our worst.

An example of God's trust. As a student of the Bible I have often been troubled by the discrepancies among the various ancient Greek manuscripts of the New Testament. There are today about 15,000 extant manuscripts, or portions of manuscripts, *handwritten*, in various libraries and museums across the world. With the invention of movable type for printing by John Gutenberg in the 15th Century, the need to copy the Bible by hand was eliminated. However, of all these 15,000 surviving manuscripts that were copied by hand, no two of them are alike! Human beings simply cannot copy without making mistakes. The great variation in manuscripts is a textual scholar's nightmare. Yet God has entrusted His written Word to us mistake-ridden humans for lo! these many centuries prior to Gutenberg's invention, even though we were unable to copy it correctly.

So He also entrusts us with His Holy Spirit. This is a clear indication of God's serious call upon our lives and His determination that the church *will* accomplish all those things which Jesus "began to do and to teach" — in spite of our faults — and we will have done them fully before the coming of the Lord.

In all humility before our wonderful Lord Jesus Christ, let us remind ourselves that Jesus said the night before He died, "He who believes in me will also do the works that I do; and greater works than these will he do, because I go to the Father" (John 14:12). Implicit within the statement, "I go to the Father", is Jesus' promise that the Holy Spirit will come to us, empowering us to do what Jesus did, and more. In what we call His Farewell Discourses, John 13 through 17, Jesus repeatedly spoke of "going to the Father", and just as repeatedly spoke of sending the Spirit, as He prayed, "..not for these only, but also for those who believe in me through their word" (John 17:20). At that point Jesus included you and me!

Do not in false humility fear to "touch" God's glory, for Jesus continued, "The glory which thou hast given me I have given to them, that they may be one even as we are one..." (John 17:22). Clearly, Jesus will honor those who obey Him. "Pride!" is the centuries-old accusation leveled by entrenched church-men at those in the forefront of every revival. But this is mere jealousy, intended to dissuade us from doing fully the will of our heavenly Father. Pride will be no problem when we abide in Jesus. "He who abides in me, and I in him, he it is that bears much fruit..." (John 15:5). "Therefore, as it is written, 'Let him who boasts, boast of the Lord'" (I Corinthians 1:31).

So let us be found to be obedient servants when our Lord returns — healing the sick, casting out demons, and proclaiming the Kingdom of God.

by Charles

God spoke words into my mind and heart which I have discovered since then were much more profound and far-reaching than I could ever imagine. He said, "Go into my Word and listen to no man and let ME tell you what I want you to know." It was obvious that God did not mean that I could not learn from others, but that He did not want me to be limited by what others said, so He could reveal new dimensions when I listened to Him.

As long as we learn only from someone else instead

of directly from the Holy Spirit, we are limited to their knowledge. We can never go beyond where those teaching us have gone. But when we go into the Bible, and listen to no man, then the Holy Spirit will let us know what He wants us to know — new revelations and unlimited dimensions.

We are not scholars or theologians but God made His Word simple about healing and so many have missed what Jesus said and did by listening to the preconceived ideas of what someone else said about how to heal the sick and who heals the sick.

We praise God for the way He opened the mind and heart of Russ Bixler and told him what *He wanted Russ to know,* even if he did have to break through the traditions of men. We do not understand Greek and Hebrew, so there are many meanings of importance in the Bible that we do not fully understand, but it is phenomenal to know that the Holy Spirit can tell any of us ordinary believers what He wants to know!

Note: All scriptures in this chapter are from the Revised Standard Version.

Chapter Six

This Could Be You!!

"Seven weeks had gone by since Jesus' death and re-surrection, and the Day of Pentecost had now arrived. As the believers met together that day, suddenly there was a sound like the roaring of a mighty windstorm in the skies above them and it filled the house where they were meeting. Then, what looked like flames or tongues of fire appeared and settled on their heads.

"And everyone present was filled with the Holy Spirit and began speaking in languages they didn't know, for the Holy Spirit gave them this ability" (Acts 2:1-4 TLB).

"Then Peter preached a long sermon, telling about Jesus and strongly urging all his listeners to save themselves from the evils of their nation. And those who believed Peter were baptized — about 3,000 in all! They joined with the other believers in regular attendance at the apostles' teaching sessions and at the Communion services and prayer meetings.

"A deep sense of awe was on them all and the apostles did many miracles" (Acts 2:40-43 TLB).

"Then Peter took the lame man by the hand and pulled him to his feet. And as he did, the man's feet and ankle-bones were healed and strengthened so that he came up with a leap, stood there a moment and began walking! Then, walking, leaping, and praising God, he went into the Temple with them" (Acts 3:7,8 TLB).

"And now, O Lord, hear their threats, and grant to your servants great boldness in their preaching, and send your healing power, and may miracles and wonders be done by the name of your holy servant Jesus" (Acts 4:29,30 TLB).

"Stephen, the man so full of faith and the Holy Spirit's power, did spectacular miracles among the people" (Acts 6:8 TLB).

"...and the Lord proved their message was from him by giving them power to do great miracles" (Acts 14:3 TLB).

"While they were at Lystra, they came upon a man with crippled feet who had been that way from birth, so he had never walked. He was listening as Paul preached, and Paul noticed him and realized he had faith to be healed. So Paul called to him, 'Stand up!' and the man leaped to his feet and started walking!" (Acts 14:8-10 TLB).

The healing power working through ordinary people like Peter and Paul has not come to a close. The real fact is, they started the church 2,000 years ago, but God's ordinary believers are going to finish this age and usher in Jesus by doing the same kinds of miracles and healings. Look at some of the spectacular miracles among the people at this first Healing Explosion in Pittsburgh.

FROM RUSSELL AND NORMA BIXLER, President of Channel 40 TV in Pittsburgh:

"Personally, it was one of the greatest ten-day

periods of my life. God really stretched my faith. I hope the same blessing happened to you, too.

"I've heard of thousands being healed in one series of meetings in Africa, or in India — but never here. Now I can say that I've seen it — right at home! Thanks so much for making it possible! How I praise God for your help!"

We asked the healing teams to write to us and tell us what happened as they laid hands on the sick, and we were inundated with the replies. Most of these letters were from people who never realized that their hands could be used by God to heal the sick! These are but a few of the testimonies written to us.

Dear Charles and Frances,

My husband and I will never be the same again because of your ministry. We read your book on healing, attended the video showings and seminars at the William Penn Hotel in Pittsburgh.

We were on the healing teams at the Civic Arena. For the first time when we prayed for people, they went down under the power. We saw legs grow, lower back pain go, two salvations, two people delivered from fear and alcohol and many others healed. We also ministered the next day at Channel 40 and saw healing take place and people go under the power. My husband was a counselor on the phone while they interviewed you and he prayed with a lady and her arm grew out at a command "in the name of Jesus" over the phone!

We were defeated Christians and were of little use in the Kingdom of God before. I was all bound up before but I'm now transformed. There is so much flowing out and like you said, healing people is so "natural." It felt like it is part of us (which it is because of Jesus in us) which we did not experience before. God's power going out of us and into others, not only His power but His love.

All that old stuff is left behind. All we can do since the 4th is walk in the new life we have found. All we want to do is lay hands on the sick and see them recover for the glory of God. We will never be the same again because of your obedience to God.

Our hearts are so full of the greatness of God in our lives and what we saw for others that was done and we are now filled with so much love as a result of your ministry in Pittsburgh.

We love and thank you so much and feel we have known you all our lives; and will continue to plant seed in your ministry because we know it is good ground. We're available to God and your ministry.

In His name,
John and Rosemary

P.S. We have relatives in Houston and are looking forward to the Astrodome!

Leg Grew Two Inches

A middle-aged man who was a guest in the audience (Channel 40-TV) came forward wearing a built-up shoe which indicated he had a short leg. I commanded the leg to grow in Jesus' name and the hip to be recreated, which had been damaged from surgery. We wept when the healing started to go through him. He cried because he knew he had a miracle and was slain in the Spirit as the pain left.

As a result of this man's healing, he was filled with the Holy Spirit. For confirmation I asked Dr. LeRoy (a chiropractor) to check him. We walked to the back of the studio to tell his wife; they needed to go shopping for new shoes immediately!   Love, Sylvia

Our faith grew as arms and legs grew!

HEALING TEAM REPORTS
"MIRACLES - MIRACLES"
Enclosed are the reports of what Alex and Christie did at the Healing Explosion. Imagine...multiply that by 1,000 and see what happened! Cannot wait until you start hearing back from the other healing teams and from the people who were healed.

It was a joy to have been in the first Healing Explosion and look forward to the next. But in the meantime, we will continue doing the works of Jesus for Jesus!
*Alex and Barb, Westminster, Md.

1. Man In Wheelchair
Symptoms: Could not walk or lift his arms to touch his head because of arthritis.
Action: Cast the spirit of arthritis out in the name of Jesus.
Result: Could find no pain, could now touch his head. Rose up and walked out of the wheelchair.
Symptom: Black Lung
Action: Commanded new lungs in the name of Jesus and instructed him to take three breaths.
Result: First breath short, second breath a little deeper, third breath was deep and the man was breathing normally.

2. Ninety-one-year-old Woman
Symptoms: Hearing aid in both ears.
Action: Asked her to remove hearing aids and commanded deaf spirits to leave the ears in the name of Jesus.
Result: Could hear even a whisper in each ear.
Symptoms: Walked with a cane because of a knee prob-

lem.

Action: Grew her legs out.

Result: She rose and walked without the cane.

3. A Young Girl

Symptom: Crooked nose.

Action: Christie laid hands on the nose and commanded it to straighten in the name of Jesus.

Result: The girl turned around to show her mother who gasped when she saw the girl's straight nose.

4. A Young Boy

Symptom: A hernia.

Action: Commanded it to leave in the name of Jesus.

Result: Neither boy nor mother could find it.

5. Three People

Symptom: Simply wanted to be blessed.

Action: Touched them in the name of Jesus.

Result: All three went down in the Spirit.

6. Young Boy

Symptom: Bed wetting problem

Action: Grew out legs.

Result: Waiting to hear.

Symptom: Had tumor on his side that was to be removed surgically.

Action: Cursed it and commanded it to wither up and die in the name of Jesus.

Result: Boy and mother both confirmed it had already shrunk to half its size.

7. A Woman

Symptom: Scoliosis.

Action: Grew out her legs and very short arm. Commanded the spirit of scoliosis to leave in the name of Jesus.

Result: A member of the healing team had a hand on the

lady's shoulder and felt the spine move and straighten.

8. A Woman

Symptom: Very bad allergy.

Action: Commanded allergy spirit to leave.

Result: She was slain in the Spirit and arose with no allergy symptoms at all.

9. Ten-year-old Girl

Symptom: Needed prayer for her eyesight.

Action: Commanded eye muscles to adjust.

Result: Improved vision.

10. Older Man

Symptoms: Diabetes.

Action: Commanded a new pancreas in the name of Jesus.

Result: Waiting for the report.

Symptom: Arthritis and pain in foot.

Action: Commanded the spirit of arthritis and all pain to leave his body in the name of Jesus.

Result: Moved his foot better. Pain had left. Led him in the sinner's prayer.

11. A Man

Symptoms: Pain in lower back.

Action: Grew out legs.

Result: Pain left his back.

12. A Man With Eye Problems

Symptoms: Could only distinguish between light and dark.

Action: Laid hands on his eyes and commanded sight in the name of Jesus.

Result: Could count my fingers in front of his eyes. Much improved.

13. Woman With Leg Problems

Symptoms: Varicose veins with numbness and pain in

legs.

Action: In the name of Jesus commanded blood to flow normally in legs along with a "Holy Spirit roto-rooter" treatment.

Result: Pain and numbness left her legs.

14. Lady With Neck Problem

Symptoms: Neck Pain.

Action: Grew out her arms and placed hands on upper discs so the power of God could adjust any of those discs that were out of alignment.

Result: Pain left.

15. Man With Glasses

Symptoms: Problems seeing.

Action: Commanded eye muscles to adjust.

Result: Improved eyesight.

*Alex is the radio engineer who saw a vision of Jesus dancing at the Pittsburgh Healing Explosion. Christie is his fifteen-year-old-daughter. His wife Barbara and daughter Donna took care of the book tables.

Short and sweet - and to the point!

1. My eleven-and-a-half year old daughter received the baptism of the Holy Spirit.
2. My husband's ulcer was healed.
3. My girlfriend's daughter had her crossed eyes healed.
4. My girlfriend's mother had a leg brace and went home without it - healed.   Brenda

Exciting, exciting, exciting!
I praise Jesus for all the excitement!

1. A lady just stood in front of me while Jesus was mending her heart.

2. Backs were healed.
3. Another lady was depressed. After laying hands on her she was better but she wouldn't leave. Finally she turned around and asked if she could lay on the floor. Praise the Lord! She wanted to be slain in the Spirit. She was! So was her brother!
4. Cancer - people were healed. I came home and laid hands on my uncle's throat for lung cancer and led him to the Lord.
5. My sister was healed of arthritis. So was a good friend of mine. Exciting, exciting, exciting!

Mary Jane

From Zanesville, Ohio

The HEALING EXPLOSION in Pittsburgh on July 4th was a great 'spiritual' experience for me. My wife was unable to attend.

Our healing team was seated among the wheelchair people, thus we began our ministry in this area. We were able to have two wheelchair bound persons to arise and walk short steps; another healed from using tobacco; another woman was healed who had eye spots, plus the laying on of hands and her 'being slain in the Spirit'; another with a sinus condition. In fact, it is now difficult to recall all the exciting happenings that took place in just a short time.

PRAISE THE LORD for the opportunity to be a part of the HEALING EXPLOSION. I'm ready for the next opportunity to participate.   Leonard

Healed in Audience

As Charles was speaking at the Pittsburgh meeting, he made a comment that people were being healed right at that moment even before they got in a healing line.

One man reported that as Charles spoke, his pain immediately disappeared. When he went back to the doctor to have his diabetes checked, the doctor told him to throw away his insulin because he was completely healed!

God in Action
What a privilege to witness *God in action*!!! I needed this as a faith builder. I have prayed for twelve years for God to heal my back, after an industrial accident. I've been manipulated, myelogrammed, massaged; I've been in traction, pumped full of procaine intravenously; I've had sound wave treatments. I've had three surgeries (fusions). My husband had to get up many nights and rush me to the Emergency Room because I was screaming and crying with pain; then a year-and-a-half ago I fell down some stairs and broke my ankle completely off from my leg and broke my leg bone also.

I have a stainless steel plate, pins and a screw in my ankle today. It hurt and swelled for one-and-a-half years until I went to the Healing Explosion at Pittsburgh, July 4th. The Healing Team sat me down and asked me to extend my legs in front of me. I had one short leg. They commanded my short leg to grow in Jesus' name. It did (Praise the Lord) but it grew out past the longer leg one-and-a-half inches and back even with the other leg, but it didn't stop... It grew back one-and-one-half inches and back out even with the other leg. The same thing happened to my arm. I felt a pulling sensation. My foot and arm never moved, they just grew. My ankle is pain free for the first time in one-and-one-half years.

I was sitting by the entry gate and witnessed people in wheelchairs leaping out of them and pushing their wheelchairs in front of them. I saw the lady who was paralyzed for seventeen years leap out of her wheelchair. The healing team tried to catch her to help her. She wobbled and cried, shouted and ran.

I was beside the young woman who *had* cancer whom they brought on a stretcher. I saw the color come into her cheeks, her foot tapping to the beat of the music, and I saw her walk with assistance!! I could feel wave after wave of love and prayers extending toward her from the people around her. I've never experienced anything like this before. God was so near. Praise His Wonderful Name!!!

"Jesus could read their minds and said to them at once, 'Why does this bother you? I, the Messiah, have the authority on earth to forgive sins. But talk is cheap— anybody could say that. So I'll prove it to you by healing this man.' Then, turning to the paralyzed man, he commanded, 'Pick up your stretcher and go on home, for you are healed!'

"The man jumped up, took the stretcher, and pushed his way through the stunned onlookers! Then how they praised God. 'We've never seen anything like this before!' they all exclaimed" (Mark 2:8-12 TLB).

Mrs. C.B.

P.S. While watching your VCR tapes, the pastor prayed for me to receive the baptism of the Holy Spirit. I fell to the floor and *couldn't* get up. My eyes were closed and I could see these "fingers of fire, flames" leaping in front of my eyes, then a pair of huge eyes looking at me. I didn't understand what was happening to me. I'm from "The Church of God" (Anderson, Ind.) church. I've never believed in this. At the Explosion in Pittsburgh *I sang in the Spirit!* I awoke in the middle of the night speaking in tongues. Woe is me — what's a Church of God

person to do? Ha.
(Editor's note — speak in tongues like Jesus said — we're from the same Church of God!)

Jesus Reigned As Miracles Rained at the PITTSBURGH HEALING EXPLOSION

FROM NEBRASKA...The three greatest things that happened through me at the Pittsburgh Healing Explosion were as follows:

1. The first person had arthritis and could not even lift her arms up halfway. I bound the devil and commanded the spirit of arthritis to come out. I told her to move her arms around and lift them higher and higher. She did it and a smile and a glow came on her face. She left happy and rejoicing that the arthritis and pain was gone instantly. *It was all done in just a few seconds.*

2. One person had several things wrong and started to tell me all of them. I told her she needed a new heart first and laid hands on her. She went out under the power. She got up saying that she felt great and thanking Jesus for a complete overhaul on everything.

3. A young man had a hip that was locked solid, a brace on one leg and crutches. After several minutes I could not see any visible results, so I called a supervisor. Even then there were no results visible. Another supervisor was called, but the man left looking just like he did when he came. We told him to keep trying to move his legs. I was concerned and wondered why he had not been healed instantly like the rest. Before the end of the meeting my concern turned to joy when I saw his leg brace laying up on the center stage right in front of me, just as if it was there to show me that

the Lord heals in different ways and that He took care of it.

Let's give God a little time!

FROM WISCONSIN: Since I have been saved most of my life, but not Spirit-filled until three years ago, I have sometimes been confused about hearing God's voice. During the three days of meetings and then the Healing Explosion I practiced Charles' suggestion of unzipping the top of my head to hear God's voice. And it worked! Before, I only thought that I could hear from God in a word of knowledge, etc. Now I KNOW that I can! Praise to Jesus!   Cheryl

ANOTHER EXCITING REPORT FROM WISCONSIN: The most exciting thing that happened to me on July 4th was the explosion of my faith in Jesus, and the kindling of a desire in me to get closer to the Lord. I want to get closer to Him like I never have before. I feel that I have a new strength to draw from not only in handling everyday problems, but in stepping out courageously to do God's work.   Wally

FROM PENNSYLVANIA: The Lord has blessed me with a miracle every 4th of July since I've become a Christian eleven years ago because I asked and always was believing. But, I never expected what He had in store for 1985.

I always knew He would bless me and bless others in the wheelchairs. This time I couldn't quite control myself, there were so many. I healed cataracts on a real old lady and the love that lady gave back to me was the greatest reward I have ever had. Not that I didn't get that from others but not quite like hers...the kisses and hugs and tears.

I healed people who hadn't walked for a long time...a lot of arthritis, cerebral palsy, a stroke, lungs renewed. One lady's leg was a lot shorter than the other. It wouldn't come out until she prayed the sinner's prayer. She wanted to dance so badly but couldn't because of the pain. She was dancing in the Spirit when I left at six o'clock that evening. Praise the Lord!   Marie

"Unforgettable successes"

How I praise and thank God for the great Healing Explosion, not only for the hundreds of people healed, but for using me (a nobody, an unheard of) to lay hands on the sick and see them healed. I didn't see Jesus at the Civic Arena, but I knew He was there because the power of the Holy Spirit was awesome.

A beautiful black lady came telling me she had arthritis and diabetes. I asked if the arthritis was hurting her at that time and where. She said it hurt all the time, that it was all above her waist, in her arms, shoulders, etc. I bound Satan and cast out the demons of arthritis and diabetes. I asked her how the arthritis was. She twisted every which way, throwing her arms in every direction, and it was completely gone. I then commanded a new pancreas to come into her body in the name of Jesus (just like Charles did for Frances.) We both thanked Jesus and claimed it done. Of course, I couldn't tell if she had a new pancreas, but the Word of the Lord came forth earlier in the service stating He was going to heal all who had hands laid on them—so I believe she received. (Jesus healed them all many times and told us we would do what He did and more, so why shouldn't it be so in Pittsburgh?)

A very nice man came to say he had pain in his arm constantly and his hand was numb. The doctors didn't know what caused it. I laid my hands on each side of his arm and commanded the pain to leave and the arm to be healed in the name of Jesus. I then asked how his arm was. He moved it all around and the pain was all gone, but his hand was still numb. I put his hand between mine and demanded the numbness to leave in the name of Jesus. I then asked about the numbness. He moved his fingers and thumb every way and it was all gone. This only took about three minutes in all. That man was absolutely stunned with amazement.

A dear little elderly lady came with an aching back, heart trouble and nervousness. When I went to sit her down to measure her legs, she couldn't see what that would do and thought I hadn't understood her problem. I convinced her to sit down and I would show her. One leg was shorter than the other and I commanded it to grow in Jesus' name and it grew right out. She was surprised to see that, and her back was much better, but said it hurt a little between her shoulders — so I measured her arms and one was shorter than the other; I commanded it to grow in Jesus' name and it did. She no longer had back problems. I then bound Satan in Jesus' name and commanded the demon of heart trouble to come out. I laid my hand on her heart area and commanded a new heart to come into her body in the name of Jesus. I don't know what happened, but she grabbed her heart area at that time. I then said "in the name of Jesus" and placed my hand on her forehead and she went down under the power — we finally had to get her up. She said she was much better. We thanked Jesus, she gave me a big hug, and left.

These three are examples of my unforgettable successes. They were all, small and large, fantastic to me. I measured so many legs and arms and commanded them to grow (they all did) that I wondered if God really wanted me to be an expert along that line.   June

People React Differently!

FROM WILLOUGHBY, OHIO: First of all we want to praise God for the chance to work with you on July 4th and to say — *"Thank You"* for showing us the revelation you have received on how to heal the sick.

A young woman came who had hemorrhoids and dermatitis. I rebuked both and gave her a Jesus overhaul. We had her raise her hands as to praise God, lightly touched her forehead and she went down under the power. She came back to us a little while later and told us she was in pain all day from the hemorrhoids and had difficulty walking, but after we laid hands on her the pain left. She came expecting and she wasn't disappointed!

A woman came who had arthritis in her shoulders. We told her it was a spirit attacking her body and being a believer, she understood. Laying both my hands on her shoulders we bound the demon and commanded it to leave. We then commanded strength to come back into the bones and commanded the pain to leave and allow her shoulders to move normally. The thing that amazed us the most was that she was jerking and shaking uncontrollably as this was going on. After all this we grew out her arms and she went down under the power.

We'd like to add one that, although it may not be a spectacular healing, it touched our hearts. He was a man in his forties that had pain in his knee. It was an annoying pain, nothing crippling, but bothersome. We had him sit down and realigned his spine and grew out his leg. Then we very simply rebuked the pain and commanded it to leave. Then we told him to move it. At first he moved it very slowly, then faster and faster. Each time he kept saying, "I got it, *I got it, I GOT IT!!!*" To see his face and hear his shout of jubilee was just as memorable as the rest.

Thank you very much and we can't wait until we stand with you again. We were with you in Pittsburgh, and then we stood with you in Akron, and we're looking forward to the next time (we're believing that in faith)!!

Your family in Christ,

David, Candi, Cristal, and Tiffiny

FROM COLUMBUS, OHIO: I was so blessed at the Healing Explosion! To see the power of God working through me to heal and set people free was the biggest and most exciting thing for me. I had never had anyone fall under the power as I laid hands on them!

The anointing was so strong I don't even remember everyone I laid hands on. I healed a lady with hypertension and the power of God hit her — a man with (I believe) back problems — and boom! The power of God fell on him. One man hugged me and just thanked me — praise Jesus!

The greatest thing Jesus did was in my husband who is born again, but not walking totally in the fulness of Christ (soon and very soon though — Glory!) He was "Mr. Critical" of healing and just about everything of the manifestation of the gifts. He was there although I didn't get to sit with him. After it was all over, he was still "picking" and I was hurt because I was so sure he would be convinced of some things.

Anyway — that night we were tired. We went to bed — the next day Paul said to me: "You know what? Something kind of strange happened to me last night."

I said, "Oh, really, what?"

He said, "I woke up PRAYING IN TONGUES!" Glory!

I was so excited, I almost didn't believe him! He had to tell me three times. He said it so calm and cool that I thought he was pulling my leg. To me, that was the biggest miracle to see my hubby who is not totally convinced of the baptism with the Holy Spirit...pray in the Spirit! I loved it! And I love you all!

To God be the Glory!   Vickie

"And these signs will follow those who believe: In My name they will cast out demons; they will speak with new tongues" (Mark 16:17 NKJV).

FROM SALEM, OHIO: How I praise God for you. I thank God for the opportunity to be used by Him in the great HEALING EXPLOSION. God used me in a mighty way that day.
1.   A large lump instantly left from a lady's left breast.
2.   A young man's shoulder popped with a loud noise everytime he moved. The shoulder went back into socket and the noise stopped.
3.   A lady's eyes were instantly healed and vision returned to normal.
4.   Ears popped open instantly and hearing restored. These people came back to me to tell me this and it was confirmed.

I have been rejoicing and thanking God for the healings.

And in my church, Pastor Bob surprised me by asking me to conduct the healing part of the service today. Emotions, a knee problem, and nerves were healed today. It was very exciting to be used by God in my home church.

Pastor Bob's been teaching us to do the Word, and finally I took that bold step of faith. But Charles and Frances, you encouraged me right up to the time and I thank God for you. I shall always hold your ministry high before God.   Connie

"And they went out and preached everywhere, the Lord working with them and confirming the word through the accompanying signs. Amen" (Mark 16:20 NKJV).

From a Michigan Asparagus Farmer

I'm still praising God for what He did at Pittsburgh! Sorry I didn't get this letter right back. I've been working — recouping from Pittsburgh financially!

I won't be in the book because nothing *spectacular* happened — well, it was to *us*! A man with a cracked rib was instantly healed as Jesus and I spoke healing to him. He felt heat and the pain left. Praise Jesus! Another woman had a lump on her lower back and it went down. Many other minor things.

Just as I was writing this a woman stopped by with a sprained thumb. I felt a real anointing as we agreed for healing in Jesus' name. Hallelujah! *Pittsburgh gave me confidence to ask people if I may lay hands on them and to go out calling on the sick.*

I was also thrilled in Pittsburgh about how expectant everyone was to be healed — and how grateful.

God bless you, Charles and Frances, for making healing simple as Jesus intends it to be. And may God truly bless all who work with you two.

                        Ruby, the asparagus lady

All Miracles Are Spectacular,
Whether They're Big or Small!

Praise the Lord that in His wisdom He led us to Pittsburgh. This was an experience and a growth in our Christian walk we shall always value and treasure. It gave us a glimpse of His glory and His deep and abiding love for us.

For several months now, we have felt His call to a healing ministry, but it took Pittsburgh, with the expectancy on people's faces and the sheer joy they experienced when they realized they were healed, to confirm that this is where He wants us to be.

We saw so many nice things happen to so many nice people, that we find it hard to single out any one thing that impressed us the most. The joy of the lady whose pain from arthritis disappeared at our touch and command — the peace and serenity on the lady who was delivered from the spirit of fear. All these things will remain clear for a lifetime.

But we feel the most thrilling thing was the little four-year-old boy who walked for the first time without braces. And to think the Lord used us to work such a glorious miracle. We can still see very vividly the sheer joy and wonder on his mother's face when she led her son away without his braces. *To be privileged to be used by God to change people's lives is all any human can ask.* Praise His name!!!

We shall be ever grateful to you for having us in Pittsburgh. Incidentally, after being with you folks for a week, we can readily see why you are known as the "Happy Hunters." We came to minister, but ended up being ministered to. I have been personally healed of obesity and since your touch and prayer, have lost thirteen pounds along with my appetite. Praise Him!!!

Thank you for allowing us this opportunity to serve

our glorious Lord.   Ray and Jan

"The Happiest Day Of My Life!"
First I want to say how really thrilled I was to be able to have been on a healing team. What a blessing, that happiest day of my life!

First miracle was when I went to my brother's to see the tapes on his VCR and before we left we asked him if we could pray for healing and he said yes. He also asked the Lord to come into his heart. PTL.

Second miracle was when I walked into that arena and I was picked as part of the healing team. Thank you, Jesus. That place was anointed.

Third was when I laid hands on a boy's chest that had a visible lump and it went down in my hand. Praise God. *I tried to act calm like I did this every day.* But I almost fainted I was so excited. What a day. I felt like I was walking on water. PTL.

I thank God for Charles and Frances Hunter and their boldness to step out in faith. PTL.

As soon as I opened the healing book I knew it was anointed. Please let me know where your next Healing Explosion will be.   Rose Mary

It's Never Too Soon!
Before the 4th the healings began. Two persons' legs grew out and three persons' arms grew out. My own arms grew out over and over again as I needed adjustment until one day I asked God to heal me once and for all. He did and now I never have pain.

There were two special instant healings on the 4th that happened by the laying on of my hands and commanding in the name of Jesus. First, a young woman had a gum disease. Her teeth were just hanging in her mouth

and she had an appointment to have them all out and
false ones put in. The Lord gave me a word of knowledge
to say, "Teeth, be firmly rooted." She fell out under the
power of the Lord. I jumped down on the floor with her
and as soon as her eyes opened, I said, "Check your
teeth!" Praise the Lord, her teeth did not move.

Second, a young man had his teeth reversed. The top
teeth were behind the bottom teeth when he brought his
teeth together. His doctor told him he was going to have
to have all kinds of work done. I commanded his teeth to
be in proper order and when we looked in his mouth the
second time, they had moved into their proper order. I
checked with him to see if he could do this himself but he
told me he had felt them move. He was healed!

Two others and myself who have read your book and
watched your tapes are teaching our Bible study. We are
sharing what you taught us and what the Word teaches
us about healing.

On Sunday, August 11, our pastor had me share in
our morning service the miracles the Lord was doing.
The Friday before that the Lord had sent a young woman
from our church to our house to be healed of back pains.
She was healed and in the service that morning, she confirmed the healing power of our Lord. Since this, people
have come to our house to be prayed for. We had a time of
healing at our Bible study and everyone who had an arm
or leg short no longer does, and a Mary and Martha Fellowship has asked me to talk at their October meeting. I
have enclosed a flyer which they make up to let others
know what the topic will be for each month.

The important part for *now* is as your message goes,
we are to do what Jesus did, we have the powers He had
and *it is for all believers.*

Our prayers are with you and we *love you both.*

Seeking the heart and mind of Christ,
Ralph and Kathleen

The description of Kathleen from the flier of Mary and Martha Fellowship:
Kathleen, former manager of Century III's Sears' Beauty Salon, is presently devoting most of her time to her husband and their seven-month-old daughter.

She is that *ordinary, peculiar, Christian believer* that Mark 16 speaks of... "And these signs shall follow them that *believe*; In my name...they shall lay hands on the sick, and they shall recover." Although filled with the Holy Spirit six years ago, she only recently had that truth made real to her while serving on one of the healing teams in the Charles and Frances Hunter 4th of July Healing Explosion.

Her exuberance will quicken your faith for what God would have for you.

"*I Wanted To Run!*"
I praise God and thank Him for choosing Pittsburgh for the first Healing Explosion, and for letting me be a part of the healing team. In your letter you asked me to describe simply the three most exciting things that happened to me there. Well, first of all, I somehow became separated from my team partner very early.

I was in the wheelchair section alone! There was a woman sitting there about fifty years old who had severe arthritis and had not even stood up on her feet in years. After binding the spirit of arthritis and commanding it to come out of her, I told her to rise and walk in the name of Jesus. Slowly she began getting up until she was standing alone, then she began to walk, rather stiffly. I called one of the marshals and told him of her healing. He said to her, "If you are healed, why are you standing so stiffly?"

She replied, "Honey, if you spent as many years sitting in that wheelchair as I have, you would be a little stiff, too." In a few minutes the stiffness left her as she kept walking and before long she and I were dancing together.

The second miracle was a man in his sixties who had emphysema and was having a terrible time breathing. As I laid hands on him he began to breathe normally and began shouting and breathing deeper and deeper. He was healed, praise God.

My third most exciting miracle was a young man who had vision problems, a throat condition and a stomach problem which caused him much pain. I barely touched his eyes and was just beginning to command perfect vision into his eyes when he was slain in the Spirit. I had not even gotten to the throat and stomach problems yet. He was under the power for about three or four minutes when he arose and began hugging me and telling me that he could see perfectly and the stomach pain was gone. He said he was going to have the throat condition checked out but he knew he was totally healed.

One of the greatest miracles I experienced was personal. I had been praying for some time to be used of God in any way He wished. When we were sitting there in the arena before the healing began, I was listening to the singers when Satan, who loves to torment the believers, began telling me, "What are you going to do when it comes time to heal the sick and all the other healing team people get results and when you lay hands on the sick and nothing happens, what are you going to do then? You are going to look like a fool. Think how embarrassing that's going to be."

Let me tell you, Charles and Frances, for one split second I wanted to run and keep on running right out of that arena, but praise God, I recognized Satan and bound him and commanded him to depart from me for I know him to be a liar and the father of lies. My God didn't bring me here for nothing. My faith soared at that point and as you read in this letter, miracles *did* happen when I laid hands on the sick.

As a result of the Healing Explosion, our church has purchased and sold fifty books "To Heal the Sick" and we will be getting the tapes soon and plan to start classes and have our own healing ministry. It was prophesied in our Sunday morning worship yesterday that our church will have a large healing ministry. I thank the Lord and I thank you, Charles and Frances, for giving me the opportunity to be on a healing team and help fulfill the great commission.

God bless you both with deep Christian love,

Joan

From Freedom, Pa. — Real Freedom!

I thank God He led me to come to the Healing Explosion at the Civic Arena in Pittsburgh, Pa. on July 4, 1985.

I have been born again since 1980 and I am twenty-six years old. Before I came down to the healing area, I had allergies to hay fever, cut grass, and pollen so bad that whenever I would mow the yard, I had such severe headaches, my sinuses would swell up so that I couldn't breathe, my eyes would burn and water so bad I had to put ice on them — that was before I came down.

Now, about three weeks after, I've mowed our grass and both our neighbors' grass several times without so much as a sneeze! I have no more headaches! My eyes no longer burn! I have no more hay fever! Praise God!!!!

Rich

"Joy Unspeakable"

What a thrill and joy unspeakable to be at the Healing Explosion in Pittsburgh, to experience one of the greatest anointings of the Holy Ghost that my wife, Betty, and I have experienced.

The power of God was so great and strong that human understanding cannot fathom the extent of its height and depth.

You two put a program together that was altogether fabulous and glorious. The singing and every facet of the whole affair was just out of this world, especially the patriotic affair. It was the greatest.

Upon returning home, the anointing continued to move in a mighty way. A call from an unbeliever in the fulness of the Holy Ghost received total deliverance from demonic pressures of headaches, mental disturbances and other pressures. She was overjoyed and continued to call us days following. Another call from a sister of a man who hasn't talked for one-and-a-half years was born again over the phone, and his only communication was an "ugh" when we talked of God's complete salvation plan.

Gordon and Betty

"I Was One of the Attendees"

Enclosed is my pledge for July for the Pittsburgh Explosion. I can't possibly think of the three most exciting things that happened to me; as each and every one was exciting. I was one of the "attackers" in the wheelchair section. My partner disappeared so I ministered with no partner other than Jesus and the Holy Spirit. I laid hands on five people in wheelchairs and, praise God, three rose up and walked instantly. (I'm totally believing for the other two!) These were no more exciting than the many other people I laid hands on. I get excited whether it be a sinus condition or crippling.

I laid hands on a seventy-nine-year-old nun and she immediately "rose" up out of her wheelchair and walked for the first time in years. Not only was a dear man delivered and healed but the Holy Spirit really took over! I commanded his tongue to be loosened — I commanded normal speech (he had flat speech that the deaf have) and, praise Jesus forever, he started speaking just as you and I do. I could go on forever.

I'm sorry to say my pastor won't allow me to share anything that happened on July 4th, but I can't be stopped to share on a one-on-one basis.

Love in Christ,   John

"Jesus led him away from the crowd and put his fingers into the Man's ears, then spat and touched the man's tongue with the spittal. Then looking up to heaven, he sighed and commanded, 'Open!' Instantly the man could hear perfectly and SPEAK PLAINLY!" (Mark 7:33-35 TLB).

"'What shall we do with these men?' they asked each other. 'We can't deny that they have done a tremendous miracle, and everybody in Jerusalem knows about it. But perhaps we can stop them from spreading their propaganda. We'll tell them that if they do it again we'll really throw the book at them.' So they called them back in, and told them never again to speak about Jesus.

"But Peter and John replied, 'You decide whether God wants us to obey you instead of him! We cannot stop telling about the wonderful things we saw Jesus do and heard him say" (Acts 4:16-20 TLB).

"Learned How To Minister Baptism
With The Holy Spirit!"

I want to personally thank you for being willing and obedient to our Lord for this wonderful Healing Explosion. As you know, many areas of our lives changed from the praise and worship also.

At the Explosion the Lord helped many in overhauling people from head to toe. Most people that came to me had lists of things wrong with them. This broke my heart tremendously because the Lord blesses my life with divine health.

One woman was delivered from smoking, another was healed of stiff knees from arthritis. Three very heavy women came to me and I suggested praying for their appestats and they received it with great tears of joy. All three women were suffering from arthritis.

The Lord has healed me also from junk-food-itis, and I have lost weight along with great motivation and exercise. I prayed for a woman with a black spot in her eye and she gave the glory to God at the arena.

At home here, things happened for me this week. For the first time I was a little (copy) Charles Hunter in ministering the baptism of the Holy Ghost. Thank you, Charles, for showing us how easy it is to minister it. Everyone who asked received. Praise the Lord!

In His Service and Love,
Emmy

Legs Pop Out!

On the 4th of July, nine of us came from Columbus and we had a beautiful time. There is so much I could relate, but I'll only tell about three of the healings in which God used me.

1. The first person I ministered to was a lady with a

lower back problem. I asked her to sit down so I could
check her legs, and sure enough, one was an inch shorter
than the other. I told her God was going to grow her leg
out, and when He did, the leg popped out real quickly
and the lady let out a yelp and said, "I didn't expect
that!"

I told her, "I did!"

2. A man with a similar problem with his back and
short leg came down to be healed. The Lord told me to in-
quire about his operation. I did and he said that he had
two discs removed. I explained that God was going to replace the missing discs and repair all the damage; then
God would lengthen his leg. I asked God to do the miracle on his spine; then I asked God to grow out his leg,
and nothing seemed to happen. The Lord told me to be
patient, He was performing major surgery. I explained
this to the man, and very slowly the leg came out and the
man walked away healed.

3. A lady came down with a severe pain in her neck
and it hurt to turn from side-to-side. From your teaching
I remembered to deal with the top disc. I went through
the procedure as I had learned, and nothing happened. I
remembered you said that if one thing doesn't work, try
another. I listened to the Lord and He said it was fear. I
cast the spirit of fear out of her in Jesus' name and she
was totally healed.   Joe

Beginning of Revival

John and I are continuing to praise God for the re-
sounding effects of the "Healing Explosion." This is
what we would call the beginning of revival. You folks
will never get a report on the full impact of the meeting
until you get to heaven. The believers are still talking
about it and the saints who didn't attend can only say

they wish they had been there.

Healing Testimonies:

1. Dumb and deaf spirit out. Girl heard and spoke her first words, "I love Jesus."
2. Arthritis gone — surgery not needed in a young lady.
3. Sugar Diabetes healed.
4. Holy Ghost brushed away cloudy haze over eyes.
5. Many arms and legs grew out.
6. Mongoloid spirit cast out.
7. Hereditary spirit cast out of adopted son.

          ....and many, many more.

God bless you and we continue to pray and intercede for your great work. You folks are special to us.

Love in Christ,   Eleanor and John

"Jesus now returned to the Sea of Galilee, and climbed a hill and sat there. And a vast crowd brought him their lame, blind, maimed, and those who couldn't speak, and many others, and laid them before Jesus, and he healed them all. What a spectacle it was! Those who hadn't been able to say a word before were talking excitedly, and those with missing arms and legs had new ones; the crippled were walking and jumping around, and those who had been blind were gazing about them! The crowds just marveled, and praised the God of Israel" (Matthew 15:29-31 TLB).

"I'm Healed!"

Being part of what God is doing in these last days is very exciting to me. Having the privilege of being on a healing team — listening as God spoke and watching as His power went through me into many as they were slain in the Spirit was awesome to me.

One boy (around 18) came up with severe pain in his

neck. I laid my hands on his neck in the position Charles showed us, commanding the pain to be gone and the vertebrae to line up straight. As I told him to move his head with my hands still on his neck, he said he heard crackling, then a very large smile formed on his face as he said with much excitement, "I have no pain — it's all gone. I'm healed!"

Praise the Lord, what excitement filled my being for him and the *glory of God!!*

I just want to thank you both for being so obedient to God. I pray for you and love you.

In His Love,   Linda

It seemed that the crowd at the Pittsburgh Civic Arena was about like those who saw Jesus doing these marvelous miracles. The members of the healing teams did not heal them all, but this was the beginning where the believers made a dynamic start, and we believe that it will not be long before we will see all the things that Jesus did happening through His body of believers in a Healing Explosion.

God is honoring the willingness of His ordinary believers to step out in obedience and trust and do the works of Jesus so the world will believe that Jesus is the way, the truth, and the life, and that through believing in Him, they can have eternal life!

PARDON ME, THE DOORBELL JUST RANG: It was a lady from a delivery service bringing the baggage which was lost yesterday on a plane trip. Just as the disciples witnessed wherever they went, I talked a moment to the lady, she recognized me from a long time past, and said she had been off work a year with a back problem and this was her second day back to work. So, between paragraphs of writing this book, I sat her down, grew out her leg as I commanded her back to be healed, AND IT WAS HEALED¹

Chapter Seven

*The " Healing Explosion"
As Seen Through The Eyes
of an Unsaved Jewish Mother*

I was delighted to learn that the Healing Explosion
was to be held in Pittsburgh, Pa. I grew up in Pittsburgh,
the only child of Orthodox Jewish parents. By the time I
left home at the age of eighteen, I had extensive education in my religion — its roots and traditions, that is. I
had thirteen years of Sunday School, five years of Hebrew school and three years of the College of Jewish
Studies...none of which led me into a personal relationship with God nor prepared me for the turbulent, rebelli-
ous years to come.

I moved into the 1960's like many of my peers — un-
happy, unsettled, undisciplined. As a college drop-out, I
dropped into the world of Haight-Ashbury, extensive
drug abuse and all the lies and deception that accom-
pany this lifestyle. Even my thirteen-year-marriage to
another drug abuser finally ended in divorce. All I had to
show for my life was a beautiful daughter. Through it all

my parents blamed themselves. They would repeatedly ask, "What have we done wrong?"

After many years of directionless searching, the prayer and loving devotion of a dear Christian friend paid off. She shared the gospel with me and patiently overruled my objections for six long months until my intellectual resistance and spirit of religiosity was broken. In November, 1981 I accepted Jesus Christ as my personal Lord and Savior.

Only another born-again Jew could know what I initially experienced. The overwhelming desire to share my new found faith and happiness with my parents remained squelched and hidden for the first few years. This was easy since I lived in California and they in Pittsburgh. My time was spent getting rooted and grounded in God's Word. By the time I was ready to confront my parents, my father was very ill. I flew to Pittsburgh but barely had the time to share with him before he expired. My mother was too upset to even listen. I flew back to California broken-hearted and guilty that I hadn't attempted to reach him sooner.

For the next year and a half any mention of Jesus or my Christianity on the phone to Mother and she quickly changed the subject. Her position was, "If it makes you happy, fine; but it's not the way we were raised." She refused to discuss it with me and forbade me to mention the name of Jesus to her. To an unsaved Jew, the name of Jesus mentioned lovingly is like a blasphemy and belief in Him is being a traitor to your faith, your upbringing and your family.

When Frances and Charles came to Word of Faith Ministry, my home church in Santa Barbara, Ca. and announced a Healing Explosion was to be held in Pittsburgh, my spirit went off like a rocket. I prayed that

God would make a way for me to attend. And make a way
He did. Not only did He open doors for me, He rolled out
the red carpet.

My letter to my boss requesting a full week off not
only met with unprecedented approval but it was an excellent chance to witness to him the who, why and where
of my destination. The expense for the flight was provided for in a love offering from members of my church. *I
was to be the Word of Faith representative to the Healing
Explosion!* On faith, I had made my plane reservation in
advance and the amount of the love offering was exactly
thirteen dollars more than the cost of the round trip
flight. The thirteen dollars was the exact amount needed
for taxi fare and tip from the airport.

My mother was absolutely thrilled that I could come
home. By sandwiching the five days off between two
weekends, I had a total of nine days to spend in
Pittsburgh. The pre-arrangement between Mother and I
was that she agreed to attend all meetings at the William
Penn Hotel prior to the Healing Explosion as well as the
July 4th Explosion itself. She wanted to be near me so
much it overrode her opposition to the nature of the
agenda before us.

The weekend after my arrival was spent visiting
family and Mother requested that I not reveal the true
nature of my homecoming to most of them. With only
three cousins was I able to share my love for Jesus (one
who I had been witnessing to through the mail and the
other, a married couple who had been very close to us
over the years). And all the while, I kept up a gentle witness to my mom leading her up to the long awaited week
to come. I had to stretch my memory back four years to
recall my initial reactions after attending my first
church service. Word of Faith Ministry is a full gospel,

strong evangelical, tongue talking, gift of the Spirit believing Charismatic church. Imagine the difference from
the solemn, pious worship services I had attended at the
synagogue all my life.

And then there were Satan's attacks every moment.
Who said he doesn't quote the scripture? He repeatedly
tried to scare me by quoting I Corinthians 1:18, "The
things of God are powerful to we who are saved but
foolishness to those who are unsaved."

I countered him back by quoting Acts 16:31, "Believe in the Lord Jesus and you shall be saved, you and all
your household." I quoted Romans 1:16, "For I am not
ashamed of the Gospel for it is the power of God for Salvation to everyone who believes, to the Jew first and also
to the Greek." As an added measure, all week I kept both
of Mother's T.V. sets tuned to Channel 40. Mother kept
closing the windows so the Jewish neighbors wouldn't
hear her listening to a Christian television station, however she did not daunt me in the least. I had waited a long
time for this opportunity.

Our first meeting at the William Penn Hotel was
Tuesday, July 2. We arrived extra early so I could get
Mom an aisle seat so she could witness with her eyes the
entire proceedings. As the meeting opened with beautiful praise and worship music, Mother could not get over
the many young people and adults literally dancing in
the aisles. She could not escape the love and happiness
we all shared not only in Christ but also to finally be present at the start of the Healing Explosion.

That night healing techniques were discussed and
demonstrated. A young woman from North Carolina
went forward to be healed of terrible lower back pain
that had plagued her for seven long years. She said she
was barely able to sit on the bus coming to Pittsburgh be-

cause of the severe pain. One of the members of the healing teams had her sit in a chair and after discovering one leg shorter than the other, commanded the short leg to grow out in the name of Jesus.

By this time my mother had scooted her chair right in the center of the aisle. Her eyes were riveted on the platform. The woman stood up and the pain in her back was completely gone. She ran down the aisles praising God and began to jump around and do things she couldn't do previously. All the while she was loudly praising God and proclaiming, "I'm healed, I'm healed."

This was followed by more praise and worship during which my mother left her chair and walked to this woman. After looking over her shoulder to make sure no one was listening, Mother gently whispered to her, "Dear, you look wonderful but tell me how do you *really* feel?"

The lady started to laugh and realizing that mother was obviously not born again, she began to hug her and love her and witness to her. I joined in and soon the three of us were praising God for her healing. God always sends the right laborers. All week, at every meeting this beautiful woman made it a point to seek Mother out to hug her and love her. Mother was so moved by this that it had a profound effect on her throughout my entire visit.

Subsequent meetings had Mom on the edge of her chair. We even met another Jewish believer there. John, a bright, loquatious young man from Pittsburgh took time to share his testimony with Mother. At one meeting, he kept looking at the two of us and finally came over. He said to my mother, "I can just see the immense love you have for each other," a remark Mother said she had waited a lifetime to hear. She repeated it to me over and over in the days to follow. She almost let John pray for her arthritic legs but was afraid she would "faint" like all the others were doing.

And on it went all week. Mother was astonished at the love abounding in the meetings and the healings she personally witnessed. By the morning of July 4th, she was up extra early packing sandwiches to take to the Civic Arena. Since I was on a healing team and unable to sit with her, I prayed God would send me someone in whose care I could entrust Mother during the day. Sure enough, He provided a woman of Mother's age who had come from Canada with her friend who ultimately became my healing team partner. I sat Mom in the very front row with final instructions to keep her eyes open because she was about to witness miracles that would far outshadow those she had already seen at the William Penn Hotel meetings all week.

My assigned seat with the other healing team members turned out to be right in front of where I had sat my mother. My partner and I prayed together and got in one accord. The opening ceremonies and the praise and worship were more beautiful than I had imagined. The culmination of months of study and preparation, the realization that Mother was opening to the gospel and the absolute magnitude of what was to come brought tears of joy during the processional.

As the time approached for those to come forward for healing, the devil reared his ugly head again. As also confessed the following morning at the Victory Breakfast by members of healing teams, I began to experience some anxiety. I half-jokingly asked God to start me off easy. "Give me the ones with a common cold; the ones who need warts dissolved," I said. Within the next five minutes assignments were given out. My partner and I had the wheelchair section!

What happened to Mother was described by her at a dinner party given by my cousins the following night. My cousin, Ryna, is a leading runway model in Pittsburgh and her husband, Herb, a top periodontist. Their son, Jimmy, a dental school student, was also present at the table. They were all anxious to hear about the Healing Explosion, especially Mother's reaction. They had already accepted my Christianity on the same grounds as Mother — "...if it makes you happy, but it's not for us."

Mother was absolutely exuberant and excited in her description of the miracles. She couldn't get over how each person on the healing team spoke with such force and authority. She was amazed how people were falling to the ground and none got hurt, but rather healed and free of whatever sickness had brought them there in the first place.

Her voice lowered and she was almost whispering when she declared that all this was being done by using "that name"! She intuitively knew that if we hadn't said "that name" then the people might not have been healed. After my younger cousin left the table to go upstairs to study, Mother then revealed that the name was "JESUS". There, she finally said it! It's hard to explain how difficult it is for an unsaved Jew to say aloud the name of Jesus — a stumbling block I, too, had to get over in the beginning.

My older cousins joined her enthusiasm. Herb asked point blank, "Aunt Lill, would you ever consider converting?"

Mother thought for a minute and answered, "Well, Herb, you know it takes me a long time to make a decision since my husband died. But I can't dispute that what I have witnessed this week were truly supernatural miracles. Who knows what time will bring."

While the dinner conversation drifted to many subjects, it was Mother who brought back the subject of the Healing Explosion several times. She told of the man whose wife pushed him into the meeting in a wheelchair. His foot was extended and he was unable to move it. She was not close enough to hear what his illness was but she could see the healing team lay hands upon him and with great authority and love command him to get up and walk. At first he was too weak, she said. Two men got under his arms and literally dragged him several steps. he was barely moving his legs. The second thrust he was moving both legs and soon he was walking totally unassisted. By the end of the day, Mom said she was astounded to see this man literally walking out of the arena pushing his wife who was riding in the wheelchair.

Mother proceeded to tell about deaf ears being opened and blind eyes seeing. Getting arms and legs to grow out was no problem, she confidently said. You can only imagine my delight.

My last few days in Pittsburgh were spent in a close, loving relationship between Mother and I, one we had never experienced in my forty-one years. We were even praying before meals in the name of Jesus. Prior to my departure for the airport, I tuned in Channel 40 on her T.V. sharp and clear. I then scrambled her reception from all the other stations. (Mom has a habit of flipping through the dials for the best reception rather than the content of the program.)

As I was about to board, Mother called me back for a last good-bye. She held out her hand with three fingers pained and affected from years of arthritis and said, "Do you think Jesus could do something about this?"

I left Pittsburgh with great hope for Mother's salvation. It is my fervent prayer that by this time, she, too, will have become a born-again Jew.   Ellie

"This illustrates the fact that Israel will be a long time without a king or prince, and without an altar, temple, priests, or even idols!

"Afterward they will return to the Lord their God, and to the Messiah, their King, and they shall come trembling, submissive to the Lord and to his blessings, in the END TIMES" (Hosea 3:4,5 TLB).

Chapter Eight

End-Time Harvest

What is the central purpose and accomplishment by the Spirit of God in the Healing Explosions?

We believe the final harvest of souls in preparation for the return of Jesus is centered around three major works:

1. *Preparing the Body of Christ* to be a holy bride, without spot, wrinkle, or blemish. "Only the holy shall see God!"

2. *The total and complete fulfillment of what is commonly called the Great Commission.* We believe this to be a prophecy which *must come true because Jesus prophesied* just before He left the earth. He told us that EVERY BELIEVER will: preach the gospel (win people to Jesus); cast out demons; speak in tongues (the baptism with the Holy Spirit); handle serpents (the old devil) and be unharmed by poisons (demon powers and their works); and lay hands on the sick and they shall recover.

3. *The Body of Christ must be in complete unity.* We believe that when every believer and all those new babies who come into the kingdom of God are out daily winning

people to the kingdom (with zeal and compassion for
souls) and doing this with signs and wonders following,
there will be no time nor thought of differences of belief
or selfish religious doctrines, but they will be so busy
obeying Jesus' prophecy that unity will be total and complete.

From the center platform in Pittsburgh we watched
over 1,000 men, women, boys, and girls, ordinary people
from all walks of life and from many denominations, step
forth in unity to accomplish one single goal—to minister
healing and deliverance to 11,000 people who came expecting. We were witnessing the end-time ministry of
Jesus' body in action as it should be every day.

As reports began streaming back to us from twenty-
nine states represented in the healing teams (as well as
Canada, Germany, and Ireland) of the phenomenal healings, both quantity and magnitude, we saw that Jesus
had accomplished another facet of the end-time ministry
of His people.

The healing teams went back to their individual
churches to testify how God had "even used me" to do
miracles. The excitement and determination to continue
this great explosion was contagious. One pastor reported
that the Sunday morning after the Healing Explosion,
several members of his church who had been on the healing teams testified for over half the service about the
scores of great miracles God did through them—just ordinary believers.

Then the pastor said, "Tonight is our regular
monthly miracle service, but I'm not going to minister.
The trained healing teams from Pittsburgh will minister
and we are going to have a 'mini-healing explosion'!"
And a healing explosion they had! As far as they could
determine, 100% of those who came for healing were

healed. That is truly the end-time ministry of the body of Christ in action.

A pastor reported that perhaps the most timid lady in his church had trained for the healing team. As she stepped out with the other teams to minister her very first healing, she thought, "God, let me have a simple one like growing out an arm for my first one!" Wouldn't you know it, God gave her a man in a wheelchair, crippled with rheumatoid arthritis. She thought, "Oh, no, God, not a hard one like that!"

However, she had listened to her teaching closely. She remembered we told her that Jesus had placed her in the position of responsibility to take back from the devil what he was putting on God's people. She was to boldly bind the devil and cast out spirits and act like she belonged to God and take authority over sickness. She remembered that she was to believe that everyone she touched would be healed no matter what their problem was.

With "timid-boldness" she said, "Devil, I bind you by the power of God's Holy Spirit, and you spirit of rheumatoid arthritis, I command you to come out in the name of Jesus." Then she said, "Now, stand up and walk in the name of Jesus!"

It shocked both her and the man when he "sprung" out of the wheelchair and began to walk. She said, "You have been able to walk before, haven't you?"

He said, "No, I haven't been able to walk for over twenty-six years!"

She was then inundated with others who had witnessed that great miracle — God working through a timid, ordinary person. They, too, wanted to be healed!

Isn't that just what Jesus said would happen?

We suggest you get your copy of "To Heal the Sick"

or "Supernatural Horizons" and carefully reread the vision we quoted in both books about what Jesus said would be the end-time ministry of the body of Christ. We know the fulfillment of that vision started on July 4th at the Healing Explosion.

We are so excited about how people from the healing teams got the message into their hearts to continue doing what Jesus did through them that day, we want to share a story that is close to our hearts, but which tells what every believer should be doing.

Our little granddaughter, Charity, now eight years old, was a member of the healing teams. We told her she had to listen to all twelve hours of video teaching, study the book like a school book and be at all the teachings in Pittsburgh at the William Penn Hotel before the July 4th Explosion. She was faithful to do everything we told her to do and she learned well. She had received the baptism with the Holy Spirit when she was two-and-one-half years old.

As we were teaching in the hotel the night before the Explosion, we had members of the teams doing the healing with supervisors showing them how, or correcting them if they went about it wrong. We worked a few minutes with Charity. We showed her that she should stand close to the people and after ministering healing, she should lay hands on them, holding her hands on them for the power of the Spirit of God to go out of her into them. People started going under the power even though she couldn't reach any higher than their chests. After we showed her a few, we went on working with others on the teams.

Suddenly, little Charity came running up to Charles, "Poppa, I did one all by myself. He had pain in his side and the pain left!"

Thursday, she was right in the middle of the 1,000 member healing team and we were told people were getting healed and falling under the power as this little child ministered "in faith". (By the way, at least one other healing team member was only six years old.)

Finally, Charity spotted an eight-year-old little girl in a wheelchair. She went to her and discovered that she had cerebral palsy and had never walked in her life. Charity remembered her instructions and teachings. She said, "Devil, I bind you by the power of the Holy Spirit. Now, you spirit of cerebral palsy, come out in the name of Jesus!" Then she said, "Now, get up and walk in the name of Jesus!"

She dragged the little girl who had never walked in her life out of the wheelchair. Charity kept saying, "You're healed, now keep walking." She had the child walk all around the arena and finally brought her to the steps leading up onto center stage where we were interviewing people who had been healed.

Joe Horst (the man God chose to coordinate this giant work) was at the foot of the stairs checking those who came to report healings before he let them come on the stage. He attempted to stop Charity and the little girl, but Charity said, "Get out of our way. I want to show Grandma that she can walk and is healed." She had the little girl (who had never walked before) walk up the steps onto the stage! Glory to God!

But that wasn't all. We were at Charity's home about a week later. A lady was helping prepare a church dinner for the next day and shared this story with us. She had arrived that morning with a lower back problem and mentioned it to Charity. Charity immediately said, "Sit down and I'll grow out your leg and your back won't hurt anymore."

But, she remembered something else we had taught her along with the other members of the healing teams. She called her four-year-old sister, Melody, and said, "Melody, I want to show you how to heal her back." (Melody had received the baptism when she was two-and-a-half years old also.) Charity said, "Hold your thumbs on her ankle bones like this; now say, 'In Jesus' name, be healed.'"

Melody did just what her older sister said and God's power from the little sister was activated when she repeated, "In Jesus' name." The leg grew out and the lady's back was totally healed.

What was the central purpose and accomplishment of the Spirit of God in the Pittsburgh Healing Explosion on July 4, 1985?

These are but a few examples and we believe they will expand all over the world as we multiplied our healing ministry by 1,000 times that single day. We pray that hundreds of other ministries will do the same and that each of those who discovered that "If Charles and Frances can heal the sick, I can heal the sick" will multiply themselves just like Charity did!

Glory to God! Hallelujah!

What a thrill it was for us to see nearly 1,000 believers who had simply been trained a few hours through our video, audio, and live teaching as well as studying the book "To Heal the Sick", step forth with authority, zeal and the power of the Holy Spirit. They accomlished what too many thought was reserved only for those who have the gifts of healing. Jesus said, "...THOSE WHO BELIEVE..."

These people ranged from six years old to the elderly, from the uneducated to the educated, from every denomination who believe in the power of God, from lay people to medical doctors and nurses, from every walk of life. When these people stepped forth in one accord with a single purpose of healing the sick and casting out devils so people would believe in the living, healing Jesus, it was awesome.

We are sharing just a few of the reports. They actually happened by the hundreds and thousands through the ordinary believer. That is the explosion which is coming NOW to the earth. Get ready to be a part of this excitement!

When we saw over half the 11,000 people in the Healing Explosion in Pittsburgh stand to receive the power of the Holy Spirit, we knew that God truly had started a new explosion to open the supernatural power to perform Jesus' prophecy that *every believer* would be used in the great harvest revival.

When the healing teams were told to move into position and start ministering healing during the Pittsburgh Healing Explosion, one person said it was as if the whole wheelchair section was attacked. Another reported actually seeing bones move. One lady got out of her wheelchair and was seen pushing her chair out the door. Nobody knew who touched her.

One woman's first "patient" was a person who walked up to her with arthritis. She was instantly healed and all pain left. Her next "patient" had arthritis and was healed. The next and the next and the next all had arthritis. She commented to one of the marshalls helping her, "I wonder why all of these have arthritis."

He replied, "You got the first one healed so I started rounding up all the people with arthritis for you!"

People from the healing teams were seen on the streets later that night ministering healing, salvation and the baptism with the Holy Spirit. The message Jesus had prophesied just before He went up to heaven was coming to pass. That was the purpose of the Healing Explosion. We believe July 4th was the very beginning of the end-time harvest that Jesus said would come. It was the birth of a new age!

One member of the teams went to the restroom after the healing time had been completed. Several people followed wanting to be healed. Truly, just as Jesus said, "...signs and wonders will follow all those who believe."

Chapter Nine

Healing Schools Are Breaking Forth

As soon as God opens the door for a Healing Explosion in a certain area, we contact churches and groups in that area to start video healing schools in their church or fellowships to train believers to be on the healing teams.

What we are seeing happen to those churches and fellowships is phenomenal and incredible. Just as the Healing Explosions cause the members of the teams to come alive to the excitement of being able to see God's power work through their hands, so it is that these healing schools not only prepare the believers to do the supernatural, but a new zeal for witnessing and a new compassion for souls is born within them.

The Healing Explosions provide an opportunity and environment where the students can put into practice what they have learned. The thrill of it all is that they don't want to quit doing what Jesus has provided for us ordinary believers, and the gospel is being spread rapidly and effectively with signs and wonders following.

Jesus summarized the ministry we were to conduct

for Him as His body in the last chapter of Mark, as well as in other places in the Bible. Putting it somewhat in today's language, He delegated the responsibilities of His earthly work to us ordinary believers and outlined what we were to do.

These schools are spreading all over the world, even when there is no Healing Explosion planned for their area at this time. Pastors and leaders are discovering that this is the very best tool available to teach their members how they can effectively minister healing and deliverance to the people in their church and community.

God has given a great tool with which to simply and quickly train people of all ages, denominations, qualifications, and personalities how to be a witness for Jesus. He said you would receive power when the Holy Spirit comes upon you, and you would BE HIS WITNESS. People discover the exciting difference in *witnessing* and in *being a witness*. The Spirit utterly compels the believers to want to change lives of others to mature them into disciples for Jesus. Instead of a duty to witness, a compassion for souls comes into their hearts, and witnessing becomes a delight through the performance of the supernatural in healings and miracles.

Our son-in-law, Bob Barker and his wife, our daughter Joan, have been so caught up with the ministry that Jesus directed us to have, that they have not only discovered the simple way of setting up and conducting a video healing school, but they have seen a dramatic, dynamic change in their church and the lives of their people, as well as people all over the great Dallas-Fort Worth metroplex.

Here is how it all began with them, followed by a simple plan whereby you can start and conduct your own school with prolific results, but without adding expensive and exhaustive work to you or your staff.

By Pastors Bob and Joan Barker
Greater Life Christian Center, Dallas, Texas

We invited Charles and Frances Hunter to start off a healing school which we were planning at our church. You don't have to have them come to start the school, but we were blessed to have this bonus!

We had advertised the meeting through our mailing list and a live call-in radio program. We were sure the meeting was going to be good but not entirely sure just how the school would turn out.

The meeting happened, the power of God was so strong and there were so many miracles that occurred that we simply cannot tell them all, however we will share one short one with you.

About a week before Christmas, 1983, Mary Beth was coming home from shopping. The streets were very icy and her car went out of control and struck a concrete base on a line pole. As a result, the car's engine was driven back into the driver's side of the car causing Mary Beth to sustain two broken ankles and a fractured right leg below the knee. The fractured ankles were known as aviator fractures...her feet were at ninety degree angles from her body. A steel plate was inserted in her right leg below the knee to stabilize that break.

Mary Beth had been suffering extreme pain and had been bedridden for approximately one year. Because of the fractures, it had been impossible to walk without excruciating pain.

Her mother and father saw Charles and Frances at a Dallas cafeteria "quite by accident" and learned that they would be ministering at Greater Life that same evening. Mary Beth's mother called and asked her to attend the meeting.

Sitting in the audience, Mary Beth was experiencing great pain and was crying. She had to walk supported by a cane. Charles and Frances asked if there was anyone present who had pain. Needless to say, Mary Beth was on her way to the front.

Charles sat her on a chair on the platform in front of the congregation and grew her legs out. She was instantly healed of all the pain. Frances then took her for a walk down on the floor level. Back and forth in front of the cheering crowd, Frances and Mary Beth walked with cane in hand shedding tears of joy and amazement after nearly two years of constant pain.

Sunday was over and Monday came. Our phone began to ring. People wanted to know more and more about how to heal the sick and what they had to do to be a part of our healing school. It was amazing. Tuesday was the same. Over and over, people called to find out about the healing school that would start that night.

Joan and I began to think that we might have twenty or thirty people at our class. We were really praying that people would have a hungering for the knowledge to know how to heal the sick. After many more phone calls, 7:30 p.m. came. People had begun to arrive at the church at 6 o'clock for the school. By the time the class got underway the first night, we had eighty-two.

Excitement was overflowing as the people sat and watched the "How to Heal the Sick" video tape by Charles and Frances Hunter. We had a question and answer time afterwards. What a blessing!

The people were so excited about learning to heal, I asked if there was anyone who needed healing. Fifteen people stood up. I had fifteen other eager beaver students stand by the fifteen who needed healing. All who needed healing were healed and many went under the power of God. We gave several an opportunity to testify. You should have heard them as they were crying and giving God all the glory!

The following week we were wondering if all of them would come back. Going to a five week class is both a commitment and real effort to many. Joan and I were both amazed as we had 103 arrive for the second class. We gave them extra instruction on healing and the healing of eyes. Five people had their vision corrected and no longer had to use their eye-glasses. Praise the Lord!

Eighty-seven graduated from our first class. Their training is going on as working disciples, doing the works of Jesus with signs and wonders following.

We averaged eighty students in our second class with sixty-five graduating. At the time of this writing we are preparing to start our third class and already have over 200 applications.

As you read on what is happening, you will see why the Good News is spreading so rapidly. Also we know that Jesus chose this as one of the very important tools to prepare the workers in the kingdom to accomplish this last great harvest of souls. Jesus said if you don't believe me because of what I say, then believe me because of the works or miracles I do.

The effects this school had on different personalities amazed us. Some we thought of as outstanding, but others we weren't sure whether they would ever be able to move into the supernatural. Aren't you glad Jesus didn't put limitations on His conditions? He just put every individual into one classification and said, "ALL BELIEVERS WOULD..."

I wondered especially about one of our graduates. She never smiled or acted excited, or at least that was the way it appeared to me from the platform.

She drove about forty-five minutes each way to get to Greater Life from her home in Arlington, Texas, which in itself was a tremendous sacrifice of not only the time, but gas as well.

Every week she came, saw and heard the video tapes of Charles and Frances and was involved in our healing lab. Week after week, she came but seemingly, no change. While Joan and I were helping her parents, the Hunters, with the Denver Healing Explosion, we got a call from this particular student, stating she was going to be there for the sessions and then the Healing Explosion on that Friday night.

She arrived and sat through the training sessions at the Coliseum, again without any great outside manifestation of excitement which would later be explained at the Victory Breakfast. That Friday afternoon the qualified healing teams for the Explosion were placed on the Coliseum floor and there she sat. Nothing happening on the outside, but on the inside of her, alarms were going off! She was growing anxious about that night when all of the people who needed healing would begin to file down to the Coliseum floor looking for her as well as the other healing teams to minister healing to them.

Suddenly, she began to think, "What am I doing? What in the world am I doing here with all these people who believe I can heal the sick? I need to get out of here. But how? There are ushers all around. Maybe I can crawl away..."

With all these things going on in her mind, it was too late. The thousands who were coming for healing were already streaming in and the service had already started.

A raging battle was going on in her mind.

The next thing she knew it was time for the people to come on the floor to be lined up and for the healing teams to take their respective places in front of the persons (patients) for whom they were to be responsible.

There in front of her stood her very first "patient". She noticed he had a milky white cloud over one of his eyes. She thought to herself, "Oh, no, it's a cataract!" Still confused as to the real purpose of her being at the Denver Healing Explosion, she remembered she was to keep her eyes open and place her hand on the eye and speak to it to be healed in the name of Jesus. She did, and as she did, something miraculous began to happen.

As she took her hand away, slowly the cataract began to dissolve and totally disappear from the man's eyes. Not knowing any of this, we went to the Victory Breakfast which couldn't have been more exciting as the different members of the healing teams began to share all of the miracles that happened through them the night before at the Healing Explosion. Joan and I were at the book table when this person who was so excited and on fire came up to the table. She was so "lit" with the Holy Spirit we almost didn't recognize her as the seemingly timid student who had been in our healing school.

She told us, "Thank you" so many times we knew that the Holy Spirit had done a tremendous work in her life. She now is setting up a video school with the video tapes in her home. She says she wants her entire church involved in healing the sick. What a tremendous blessing she'll be to those in her Bible study and her church.

Let Tyra tell you what happened.

Extension Through Believers
Through Other Believers

About three months ago, the Lord directed me to attend your healing school. I could not understand why He would send me so far from home, but I obediently followed His command. I am so glad I did. It was a life-changing experience, just like you said it would be.

I now understand that the gift of healing, as well as all the other gifts of the Spirit, are resident within each Spirit-baptized believer. Also, it is our responsibility to exercise these gifts, and the Holy Spirit will use them as He desires.

When I was first Spirit-filled, I believed that God could do anything through me. But as time passed, and I was taught that we did not receive all the gifts, I no longer believed, and God, therefore, could do nothing through me. That is why He sent me to your school. Also, I was to share the good news with those around me who are experiencing the same discouragement I did.

After completing the healing school and gifts of the Spirit teaching, I asked God to make a way for me to attend the Denver Healing Explosion. I know you will not be surprised, Pastor Bob, that He opened all the doors and even blessed me with two free hotel rooms at the Holiday Inn, Downtown.

God healed many as my team partner and I ministered that night. A man almost blind in one eye because of cataracts received perfect sight. A man deaf in one ear was able to hear. A woman with scoliosis, sway back and several spinal injuries, was healed as her arms and legs grew out. While she was under the power, I believe God also healed her pituitary gland and brain injury. A woman with a massive infection in her female tubes testified that all the pain left her after being ministered to. There was a healing of arthritis, also, and many back healings as arms and legs all grew out. Praise be to God.

Needless to say, following my report, my Bible study group is anxiously waiting to view the healing school video. I know that the Lord has prepared their hearts to receive all He has for them, that He may be glorified.

Words cannot express my appreciation to you. I know you are changing the lives of many in obedience to what God has called you to. May God richly bless you.

Yours in Christ, Tyra

There is No Limit to Benefits

Greater Life Christian Center has had a face-lift since we started a video school with Charles and Frances Hunter's "How to Heal the Sick" video tapes and their book "To Heal the Sick". Little did we realize what would happen to our church and the lives of our people.

Along with the video, we have live training and allow the students to minister healing to one another as a part of the class. They are utterly amazed when God's healing power flows through their hands and all kinds of healing take place. This has had such an impact that the students have become excited about boldly venturing out to friends and even people they don't know.

Jesus said this Holy Spirit power received through the baptism with the Holy Spirit would enable you to become a witness for Him. That's exactly what happens when a person learns how to heal the sick...he or she *becomes* a witness!

When we announced the video healing school on our weekly radio program, more people from all over the Dallas/Fort Worth Metroplex came than regularly attend our church. Christians are hungry to know how to do the supernatural. The Bible says signs and wonders will follow the believers, but some become discouraged when healings happen only occasionally. After attend-

ing the twelve hours of video, studying the book and seeing it happen through themselves, a whole new world
opens. Suddenly, they are "wild" to perform the works of
Jesus!

We were also surprised at the number of Spirit-filled
believers who were not involved with any church. After
attending our second school and one six-hour course on
"How to Develop the Gifts of the Holy Spirit", many of
the "unattached" students have become stable workers
in our church.

From these schools came another unexpected, unusual outreach for our church. Listeners to our radio
program were invited to call in if they needed healing.
Our outreach minister quickly matched the zip code area
of the caller with members of our healing classes who
lived in their area. Suddenly, a new ministry was
born..."Supernatural House Calls"!

When the trained healing teams make an appointment to see the sick in their homes, faith explodes both in
the amazed sick people who can hardly believe this could
happen to them (and it's free), and the healing team
members who have a golden opportunity to be a "doer of
the Word."

People visited are getting saved, baptized with the
Holy Spirit, delivered of bondages of fear, depression
and loneliness. Fantastic healings occur including
cancer, arthritis, back problems, internal problems, pain
leaving their bodies, etc. Truly they are doing the works
of Jesus with a new-found boldness, zeal and compassion.

God is teaching people to heal people and con-
sequently, He is bringing the body of Christ into maturity. No longer is healing a theory, instead it is becoming
an effective supernatural tool for building the kingdom

of God through ordinary believers.

Members of our church are now conducting video healing schools in other cities and churches around the Metroplex area.

As a pastor of a growing church here in the Dallas-Fort Worth Metroplex area, I would strongly encourage all pastors to start a healing school in your church using the "How To Heal The Sick" video tapes by Charles and Frances Hunter and their book "To Heal The Sick." It has done more for our church to date than having any outside speaker or singer, and more than anything that ever happened to us to bring into being the "Twentieth Century Acts of the Believers."

Chapter Ten

The Supernatural of God!

Prior to the Healing Explosions, we go into the area to hold miracle services to encourage people that "If Charles and Frances can do it, you can do it, too!" Amazing miracles happen as we demonstrate God's healing power, and then let others do the same.

The First Assembly of God in Fort Myers, Florida was charged with the power of God because of the faith and expectation of those people involved combined with some fabulous praise and worship.

As we were introduced, God spoke in an unusual way and we started off quoting the scripture, "Not by might, nor by power, but my spirit, saith the Lord of hosts" (Zechariah 4:6 KJV). Then we continued, "And my speech and my preaching was not with enticing words of man's wisdom, but in demonstration of the Spirit and of power that your faith should not stand in the wisdom of man, but in the power of God" (I Corinthians 2:4,5 KJV).

We had seen a woman being assisted up the steps into the building who was obviously in extreme pain. As

soon as we quoted the above two scriptures, we called the
woman forward. She came up on the stage and shared
about the tremendous back pain that she was having.

First, we grew out her legs and arms, then we laid
hands upon her neck and commanded the spine to be
healed. She was totally and completely and instantly re-
lieved of all pain. Her healing was miraculous, but as she
explained the rest of her story, the miracle grew and
grew.

She told of the years of pain that she endured. It had
gotten so bad that she decided she could stand it no
longer. Even though she was a Christian, she had decided
to go down to the freeway and throw herself in front of a
fast speeding car. As she was standing on the freeway,
God gave her a verse of scripture which said, "I will
never leave you nor forsake you."

She turned away from the freeway and shortly met
some people who brought her to our miracle service that
night where she was totally and completely healed!

What a way to start off a service!

Charles got a word of knowledge which was shared
by both of us...someone had tremendous pain in a collar
bone, with a possibility that the bone was even broken. A
man answered the call and we were shocked when we
saw him coming forward with his arm in a harness. It
looked like a sling, but it went around his entire body. He
told us that he had fallen out of a tree and broken his collar bone and injured his ribs and groin.

Charles asked him if he was in pain. He replied,
"Yes, intense pain!"

Charles said, "I'm going to show you how easy it is
for you to learn how to heal the sick." We asked for a believer who spoke in tongues who had never healed anyone. A young lady came up who had the baptism for four

months but had never healed anybody. She was saved when she was a young girl, but then backslid until she had recently come back to the Lord. She had never laid hands on the sick.

Charles instructed her what to say and where to place her hand. When she took her hand away, the man said, "It doesn't hurt anymore!" He proceeded to take off the sling, the harness and every bit of apparatus that he had on. He joyously lifted his arm in the air and praised and thanked God for what He had done.

We had another believer come up for the laying on of hands for the healing of his groin and ribs. We had him sit down and this believer who had never laid hands on anybody before grew out his leg and commanded the groin and ribs to be healed. He squatted down and got up...again and again. He turned to us and said, "I have not been able to do this for years."

While this was going on another interesting thing was happening. The minister of music leaned over and whispered to me that the choir was leaving on Tuesday for Europe for seventeen glorious, exciting days of singing in various churches all over Europe. The man with the broken collar bone was a member of the choir, but his doctor had said under no circumstances could he travel with this broken collar bone. As you could well imagine, he was tremendously disappointed.

Now he was healed and still couldn't go because there wasn't any room for him. The minister of music then said, "Someone called me today and said they couldn't go on the trip and could I find somebody to fill in for them." God had opened an opportunity not only for him to be healed, but also for him to go on the tour with the choir to Europe.

"Take delight in the Lord and he will give you the

desires of your heart" (Psalms 37:4). You have no idea of the joy that came when the minister of music told him that there had been a cancellation and now that he was healed, he could go as he had originally planned. He was ecstatic!

Shortly after we returned home, we received a letter from Pastor Deaton, as follows: "Greetings in the name of the Lord! Thank you for coming and sharing with us in the ministry God has given you.

"You will be interested to know that Richard Donlin, the gentleman with the broken collarbone who was wearing the brace, went to the doctor on Monday and requested x-rays. The first x-ray showed no broken bone. The doctor refused to accept that and after further discussion, took more x-rays. These x-rays once again showed bone perfection."

We were sharing the story at the Lakeland Healing Explosion when suddenly a voice came from the balcony, "I'm here, I'm here!" Richard Donlin came onto the stage and shared all that had happened to him, and then sent us a letter giving the details of the awesome miracles God had done for him in that one special moment of time!

Richard's Story:
Dear Charles and Frances,

Greetings in the name of our Lord Jesus Christ! Mrs. Pat Ladd who is from Ft. Myers Beach, Florida and a member of your healing teams at both the Lakeland, Florida and the upcoming Denver Healing Explosion urged me to write you this follow-up letter.

You will recall that I am the man with the fractured right collarbone, bruised right ribs and right groin that was healed on September 7, 1985 when you were here in Ft. Myers. There is a story and two pictures in your cur-

rent Partners' Newsletter. Also, I was in the balcony at
The Carpenter's Home Church on November 5, 1985 at
the Lakeland, Florida Healing Explosion and you called
me to the front to tell the 9,500 plus people part of my
miracle. Praise our Lord!

Let me share my amazing story. I accepted Jesus
about thirty years ago (November, 1943) in Benton, Ar-
kansas (Mt. View Missionary Baptist Church). I received
the baptism in the Holy Spirit on November 16, 1982. I
am well educated, B.S.E., M.Ed., Post Masters Degree
work and a J.D. (law degree) from the University of
Miami. I have been a teacher, a university professor, in
administration in local, state and federal programs and a
lawyer since 1976.

On August 29, 1980, I was driving home from a groc-
ery store in my sports car when another car ran a stop
sign striking my car broadside on my driving side. My car
was a total loss. I sustained head/brain injuries, broken
ribs and toes along with injuries to my neck, back, right
leg and both wrists. Before long I developed seizures,
narcolepsy (a type of uncontrollable sleeping sickness),
traumatic arthritis, memory loss, hearing loss, speech
impediments and vision problems.

I returned to work several months later but could
not work full-time nor do the same quality of work. Finally, following medical and professional advice, I began
a leave of absence on August 28, 1981 and moved to
Sanibel Island. Soon after moving, I developed ulcers,
weight loss and began using a cane (right knee). Although I hardly ever took more than aspirins once in a
while before this accident, I was taking eighteen to thirty
pills a day (nine Dilantin for seizures), (six to ten Fiorinal
or other pain headache pills), (four Tagamet for ulcers),
(three Rufin for arthritis), (three Ritalin for narcolepsy),

and (four Tranxene for my emotions). This was an expense of $150.00 to $200.00 monthly. From August, 1981 to July, 1983, I drove very little and did little physical or mental work. I was under regular treatment of at least two doctors.

On July 15, 1983, I offered to drive because my wife was sleepy after two hours of a three hour car trip. Fifteen minutes after I was behind the wheel, (my wife and son strapped and asleep in the car with me), we were rear-ended by a car pulling a heavy sailboat. My left shoulder was injured with further injuries to my neck and back. My nerves were shattered. I began regular treatment with a chiropractor.

Sometime in late 1982, I received the baptism in the Holy Spirit and I never lost faith that someday I would be "healed." In 1983 we began attending the First Assembly of God Church in Ft. Myers and I became a member of the choir in 1985. In May of 1985, I began preparing for the European choir to tour ten or more churches in France, Switzerland and Belgium from September 22 to October 7, 1985.

However, I fell off a ladder on a tree on July 27, 1985, (following tropical storm Bob) and fractured my right collarbone, bruised my ribs and groin. On August 29, 1985, my orthopedic doctor said I could not go on the choir trip because of the fracture which would require the surgical insertion of a metal plate and screws. He put me in a harness and sling apparatus to return in three weeks for a pre-surgery check-up.

But Jesus intervened and I was healed!!

On September 7, 1985, someone canceled their plane seat on the European choir trip and my healing put me back on the plane to witness more than 100 answer the altar call message in French by my music pastor, Bert

Phagen. My testimony was given in French.

In the past two months, I have not taken any medication. I did not have adverse reactions. I have had no seizures or narcolepsy attacks. I have had no ulcer problems and eat ALL foods without adverse effects. Arthritis and stiffness are gone. My vision, hearing, memory and comprehension are healed. Headaches are gone. Limping and stumbling are gone.

Now you have the full story on my healing. I will never forget what my faith and the Happy Hunters did for me on September 7, 1985. Also, my healed collarbone was confirmed by x-rays on September 12, 1985 and again by x-rays by a different orthopedic surgeon today, November 11, 1985. To God be all glory and praise!

I was glad to testify to my healing and your ministry at Lakeland, Florida, November 5, 1985. My family and I plan to attend your proposed Healing Explosion in Jacksonville, Florida in February, 1986. However, if you want me to give a testimony in Denver, I will come one day at *my expense*. I love you both and will continue to support your ministry prayerfully and financially.

Gratefully Yours,   Richard

The next morning after the dramatic service in Fort Myers, we went to Odessa, Florida, where we were privileged to watch the miracle-working power of God in one of the most unique healings and response to God that we have ever witnessed.

We were sharing excitedly about the next Healing Explosion being in Lakeland, Florida on November 3rd when a man shouted from the back of the church, "No, it's not, it's going to be tonight in Odessa! "

Some valuable lessons can be learned from this unusual testimony. George Higgins came *expecting* a miracle. He did not come to be a scoffer or a skeptic, he came expecting! We often minister to the people in wheel- chairs last because their faith has an opportunity to grow during the service as they watch other miracles. When George came forward with a group of people who were in intensive pain, we almost forgot him because his wheel- chair was placed where we could hardly see it. We also did not realize that there are times when multiple sclerosis can be extremely painful.

Charles ministered to him first by growing out his arms and legs. Then he laid hands on him and com- manded the foul spirit of multiple sclerosis to come out of him.

George began to shout, "I've got a new body! I felt it! I felt it! I felt it!" and as Charles commanded him to walk in the name of Jesus, he literally leaped out of the wheel- chair! He began to run and to jump in a most extraordi- nary way. He hugged Charles and then he ran up on the stage and hugged Frances, and then he did something we have never seen anyone else do in all of our years in the miracle ministry! He went back down off of the stage, fell to his knees, lifted his hands to the heavens and began praying to God saying, "Thank you, Father! Thank you, Father! Thank you, God! I praise you for what you have done!"

Never in all of the thousands of healings which we have witnessed have we ever seen an individual fall to their knees and begin to unreservedly praise God for what He had done. He continued this for somewhere be- tween five and ten minutes of the most emotional mo- ments I have ever spent in my life. Just to see a man take time out to thank the One who made it possible was a real heart-throbbing experience for everyone there. We could not help but think of the story of the man at the

Gate Beautiful who went walking and leaping and praising God. We have never seen anyone praise God as much as George did!

"Now Peter and John went up together to the temple at the hour of prayer, the ninth hour. And a certain man lame from his mother's womb was carried, whom they laid daily at the gate of the temple which is called Beautiful, to ask alms from those who entered the temple; who, seeing Peter and John about to go into the temple, asked for alms.

"And fixing his eyes on him, with John, Peter said, 'Look at us.' So he gave them his attention, expecting to receive something from them.

"Then Peter said, 'Silver and gold I do not have, but what I do have I give you: In the name of Jesus Christ of Nazareth, rise up and walk.'

"And he took him by the right hand and lifted him up, and immediately his feet and ankle bones received strength. So he, leaping up, stood and walked and entered the temple with them — walking, leaping, and praising God.

"And all the people saw him walking and praising God. Then they knew that it was he who sat begging alms at the Beautiful Gate of the temple; and they were filled with wonder and amazement at what had happened to him" (Acts 3:1-10 TLB).

After praising God, George began to get up. Everyone's eyes were glued on him because a person with multiple sclerosis cannot get up off the floor by himself. When he quickly rose up from the floor, he grabbed a Bible and began to run all the way around the church screaming, "I've got to preach! I've got to preach! I've got to preach!" As he continued to praise God, he ran around the church, not once, but twice, waving his Bible in the air.

Services can get wild and exciting when the Spirit of God moves!

His children had never seen him walk normally, so you can imagine what a thrill this was to his wife and children to see their daddy running around the church.

Interestingly, he had gone to a Methodist church all of his life, but just four weeks before we held this meeting, God spoke to him and told him to go to this Full Gospel church. As a result of his obedience to God, he was totally and completely healed!

The next day he slept until noon because he was so exhausted from all the running, but when he did awaken, he went swimming for two hours. On the fourth day George Higgins was on television with us in Clearwater, Florida telling the world of the mighty acts of God!

But he got the message of what all Christians should do! On September 8th he was sitting in a wheelchair, but on November 5th he was healing the sick at the great Lakeland Healing Explosion. He is putting his story into action!

Chapter Eleven

The Second Explosion

The Carpenter's Home Church

Lakeland, Florida

This is the hour of the believer! It is not the hour of the evangelist, teacher, prophet, pastor or apostle, but this is the hour for the believer to shine.

The great 10,000 seat Carpenter's Home Church in Lakeland, Florida was the scheduled site of our second Healing Explosion. Many wondered if God would repeat what He did in Pittsburgh. Pastor Karl Strader and his wife, Joyce, were the first to get the vision just a few weeks after we had made arrangements for the first Healing Explosion. They asked us to hold one in their church, and we set the date.

Video healing schools began springing up all over Florida. WCIE radio station (owned by Carpenter's Home Church) daily plugged what was happening there and as we visited church after church with miracles, the number of healing team applications grew.

We were so excited about what God was doing, we called into the radio station every morning during the final week and shared our enthusiasm with them. We called from airports in Boston, Massachusetts, Pueblo, Colorado, Pittsburgh, Pennsylvania and many other places to keep in touch with those who were hungering to see and be a part of a living God who still heals today.

"His Power Through You" is the theme of all of our Healing Explosions, to teach the believer the incredible potential that God has placed within each and every Spirit-filled believer. With the baptism of the Holy Spirit comes the same resurrection power that raised Jesus out of the grave. There is only one Holy Spirit, and the Spirit of God that brought Jesus up is the same one that indwells you and me. What an awesome responsibility God has placed upon the ordinary believer!

Even though we were shocked with the more than 1,000 believers who turned up in Pittsburgh to be on healing teams, Lakeland surprised us even more. It is a small inland town in Florida with a population of approximately 41,000 and a church sanctuary that seats 10,000. We scheduled pre-explosion meetings in many churches in the area where we saw hungry people wanting to put into effect the work that Jesus said we would do.

As the excitement continued to mount with God placing in the hearts of believers a hunger to be on a healing team, the Carpenter's Home Church decided to show the video tapes for six hours on Thursday and Friday nights for those who had not been able to qualify previously, and then decided to show them for twelve hours on Saturday. We personally wondered if anyone would come and sit for twelve hours to watch video to learn how to heal the sick. To show what is happening in the body of Christ today, more than 475 people came to spend twelve hours in one day learning! They came, brown lunch bags and all and spent the entire day to prepare themselves for what was to come.

When we walked into the Carpenter's Home Church for the first service, it was like walking into a mammoth cocoon of faith and power. There was such a feeling of anticipation in the air it felt as if you were walking around with your finger in an electric socket! The first night approximately 5,500 to 6,000 people attended in preparation for the great explosion night. Many were healed and over 1,200 received the baptism with the Holy Spirit, and the actual Healing Explosion hadn't even started yet!

The first training session on Monday morning brought somewhere in the neighborhood of 1,500 people hungry to be taught how to heal the sick, and swelled to more than 2,000 people desirous to do God's will! God is moving on people!

During one of the daytime meetings, an exciting word from the Lord came out.

"And my son and my daughter...I have even called thee to teach the masses this truth. Yea, I say unto thee, that thou art in preparation. Yea, and each life that thou toucheth is in preparation, for the day shall come when thou shalt stand and by satellite thou shalt conduct a Healing Explosion that will encompass the entire nation of the United States. Thou shalt stand in one location, yea, and thou shalt speak forth the anointed word that I have placed on thy heart and in every county of the nation, there shall be those that reach their hands forward in that local area and there shall be an explosion that is not in just one city or metropolitan area, but it shall be a

*nation-wide explosion, in one day at one time and it shall
devastate the work of the devil, thus saith the Lord."*
Are we capable of understanding the enormity of
that word? Is it possible that a sovereign work of God
could devastate the work of the devil? Who are we to not
believe God? Our hearts burn within us to train more and
more people. How is God's Word going to be spread
through the world? We believe it will be through millions
of ordinary believers who get so turned on and so tuned
in to Him that nothing else makes any difference. When
they know that signs and wonders will happen wherever
they witness the gospel of Jesus, then the billions on
earth will be touched by believers.

We've all heard that if you start with a penny and
double it every day for a month, you'll be a millionaire.
We decided to try it with souls!

Here's an interesting little thought for you. If each of
us went out and multiplied ourselves every day in God's
kingdom and the one we led to Jesus did the same thing,
in one month's time 1,073,741,824 souls would be won to
the kingdom. In 34 days, 4,750,000,000 souls, or the entire world could be reached for Jesus. Think about it!

1 day	1 soul
2 days	2 souls
3 days	4 souls
4 days	8 souls
5 days	16 souls
6 days	32 souls
7 days	64 souls
8 days	128 souls
9 days	256 souls
10 days	512 souls
11 days	1,024 souls
12 days	2,048 souls

13 days	4,096 souls
14 days	8,192 souls
15 days	16,384 souls
16 days	32,768 souls
17 days	65,536 souls
18 days	131,072 souls
19 days	262,144 souls
20 days	524,288 souls
21 days	1,048,576 souls
22 days	2,097,152 souls
23 days	4,194,304 souls
24 days	8,388,608 souls
25 days	16,777,216 souls
26 days	33,554,432 souls
27 days	67,108,864 souls
*28 days	134,217,728 souls
29 days	268,435,456 souls
30 days	536,870,912 souls
31 days	1,073,741,824 souls
32 days	2,147,483,648 souls
33 days	4,294,967,296 souls

In just 34 days — More than 4,750,000,000 souls! — All the world!

*It is estimated that there are 113,000,000 Spirit-filled believers on earth today. It would take only seven days for every soul on earth to be reached individually for Jesus if each Spirit-filled believer would double himself daily! Nothing is impossible with God!

The training continued, and the hunger in the hearts of people grew to do more and more for the Lord. Physicians and chiropractors joined with us in training the believers how to heal the sick and in turn found themselves more turned on to supernatural healing than they had ever been in their entire lives! One chiropractor said, "I have learned more here than I did in ten years of schooling!"

Pastors of all denominations came to the meetings, not bound by denominational barriers, but hungry to see what God is doing. People from all denominations were represented on the healing teams. During all the training sessions, miracles were taking place in the lives of believers.

A pastor came up to us in the hall and said, "I need to be delivered of a spirit of religion!" I IMMEDIATELY laid hands on him and cast out that spirit. Not only was he delivered, his neck problem was also healed!

The next morning we met him at the Waffle House for breakfast and later that day, he handed us the following note:

November 5...10 a.m.
Guess what happened at the Waffle House this morning? I'm the Assembly of God minister who sat with you. Remember the young man that was sitting with you?

When you left, you gave him your flyer. When he saw your picture in the flyer, he said, "That was the Hunters! Wow!"

He began to tell me about his legs...that they continually pained him...that he spent much money on special shoes, etc.

So I stood up and told him to face the aisle and give me his legs. One was about one inch shorter. I healed his legs — they became normal right in front of the onlookers and waitresses. Then I lengthened his arms and healed his neck. I told him to get up and walk and test his legs. He began to cry as everyone, including two policemen, watched. A waitress asked when the meetings were

scheduled...she wanted to come.
Praise God!! I've been released from religiosity!

Roy W.

Another letter just came in from this pastor which said, "I'll never be the same again! My eyes and understanding have been opened and I'm so excited. I FEEL LIKE I'm going to explode for Jesus. Doesn't sound very religious, does it?

During your school in Lakeland I was launched like a rocket into the middle of the most thrilling move of the Holy Spirit I've seen in the thirty-eight years of my ministry. For the last three or four months I've been praising God during my daily praying for allowing my faith to ride the crest of the mighty wave of the supernatural power of the Holy Spirit which I believe is sweeping across the nations of the world. I thank the Lord for allowing me to be a part of the fruit of your ministry to the body of Christ. I'm expecting mighty things to happen from here on, till Jesus comes!"

Came the great night in Lakeland. Pastor Strader got up to open the meeting, and there was a crack of power so loud it literally exploded in the building which had over 9,500 people in attendance. Listening to it on video, you can hear the "thunder of His voice" and we understood why God wanted us to call these meetings "explosions"! That is literally what happened! Excitement ran high as the praise and worship started off the meeting.

After worship, the glory of God was so powerful many people were healed just being in the presence of God. The Lord impressed us to read from the book of Acts:

"Now, Lord, look on their threats, and grant to Your servants that with all boldness they may speak Your word, by stretching out Your hand to heal, and that signs and wonders may be done through the name of Your holy Servant Jesus. And when they had prayed, the place where they were assembled together was shaken; and they were all filled with the Holy Spirit, and they spoke the word of God with boldness" (Acts 4:29-31 NKJV).

We asked God to literally shake the walls of that great church as we ministered first salvation and then the baptism with the Holy Spirit. And shake they did. The entire front of that great auditorium was completely filled with some 3,000 people coming for the power of God in their lives, and the aisles were filled all the way to the back of the auditorium. It was truly a demonstration of God pouring out of His Spirit today in the twentieth century.

The healing teams seated in the great auditorium reminded us of race horses waiting to be released. A woman with twelve incurable diseases was healed from a stretcher-like bed of affliction and danced all the way across the front of the church. God was preparing the hearts of those there to receive their healings, as well as those who had come to heal the sick!

Finally the healing teams were freed to encircle the great hallway completely surrounding the church, and then the sick were released to go and be healed.

Almost immediately, those who had been healed began streaming up to the stage to share what God had done in their bodies! The lines continued to form, and up until almost midnight, people were waiting anxiously to tell how God had healed them.

Here are some "Acts of the Believers" to show the different types of healings God did, right from the lips of those who received. As we report some of the miracles, you will read about them going into a room to have legs grown out. There were no chairs in the hallway, so people with lower back problems were instructed to go into a large room where they could sit down and have their legs measured and grown out.

Some Of The Testimonies from the Stage
The Night Of The
Lakeland Healing Explosion

"I had a bad car accident and dislocated a disc in my spine. The team that was upstairs...they were anointed by the Lord and ministered to me. And the Lord healed me. I have had this problem since 1975." (Woman)

"Forty-eight years ago I was running down a hill and a clothesline hit me. My spine...it's supposed to sit like this. In this area it's straight...I had spurs where it had tried to heal itself, curvature of the spine. I went to one chiropractor and he wouldn't even touch me. But there was some man who just demanded that I be healed. And my spine jerked from the top of my head...it just went in sections just like that all the way to the tailbone. My hip just rolled over. He grew my arms and legs out. I was knock-kneed, bow-legged and pigeon-toed. I took so many aspirins as a child I had bleeding ulcers. Now I'm healed and straightened up! Praise the Lord!" (Woman)

"I had a broken leg on May 24th. My back was broken in three places. I have been in a lot of pain. Just an average person on a healing team touched me. I can bend and turn with no pain now. You can have my crutches." (Man)

"I had a broken shoulder from a car accident. I couldn't move it around. A couple of women told my shoulder bone to knit together. Now I can lift my arm way up." (Woman)

"He delivered me from a spirit of cancer. I have been having a lot of problems with my lymph system. I didn't have pain tonight, but quite a bit of swelling. The swelling is disappearing. I'm healed." (Woman)

"I had two steel pins in my hand. She came over and she grew out my finger about a fourth of an inch. I could feel the steel pins before...now I can't." (A little girl with only three fingers.)

"I've had a lot of tension headaches. I had my eyes prayed for and I was healed. The pain is gone. They worked on my neck like you taught them. My vision is a little blurry but the pain is gone. (We touched her eyes.) Now the blurriness is gone. My brother was saved last night on the telephone...he pushed away his cigarettes and alcohol." (Woman)

"I've had rheumatoid arthritis for twenty years. The pain was bad tonight. I haven't been able to move my knees or walk on my feet without pain for a long time. I'm healed!" (Woman)

"Small boy born with scoliosis...straightened the back up. Dyslexia...believe it was healed."

"I was healed of a damaged jaw from a car accident. They had fixed everything but the joints. The healing team touched my jaw and all the pain is gone...I can move it around normally now."

"We're both delivered of smoking."

"I've been a diabetic for about eleven years. I walked in here tonight with a cane, my legs were both numb and I've had hemorrhaging in the eyes. Jesus blessed me and healed me with all His love. The hemorrhaging is gone. My legs are stronger and there is no numbness anymore. I have to get used to walking normally. I'm going home to ride my bike and Friday I'm going to the doctor to show off my new pancreas." (Man)

"I had spurs on the bottom of both of my feet, on my spine, on my neck...I had a bad heart valve, sugar diabetes, and bad eardrums. I just got healed of all that." (Woman)

"Every once in awhile I would have pains in my legs. I went up to one of the women in the lobby and she just healed me. She grew out my legs and my arms and my legs are just healed. I got the baptism in the Holy Ghost two years ago when I was ten. I'm going out to heal the sick now." (Girl)

"I had a clicking in my jaw for two years. While the man was ministering to me, his wife said she felt an intense heat in my back. I didn't recall any pain in my back, but I did remember the past couple years...when I turned my neck, I had a grinding in my neck that I thought was normal. There's no grinding and my jaw has stopped clicking and they grew out my arms. They ministered to my jaw...then my arms...my jaw clicked for about fifteen minutes after they ministered to me. I was moving around and kept saying, 'I know that I'm healed. I receive this healing.' I began to hurt and then I felt an intense tingling...shortly after that, it was gone. It took about fifteen minutes and I was healed." (Man)

"Well, I had a very bad back and I was led to the Lord really through my chiropractor. I received healing tonight. I had a cataract in my left eye. Everything is so bright and beautiful. Oh, there's my chiropractor!" (Woman)
(Her chiropractor) "She's clear as a bell!"

"One of the believers laid hands on me. I've been healed of a hernia that I've had for ten years. The Lord healed me tonight. One of the believers just laid hands on me and I was slain in the Spirit. Now, I'm healed." (Man)

"Systemic lupus, diabetes, heart trouble, blood pressure problems, ulcers,...the doctor told me I had eight major things wrong with me and I can't remember all of it. I'm healed."

(Healing team member about a young boy.) "He has never talked, never heard. He uses hand signals. He says the noise is getting louder. He was born deaf and never been able to talk. When I put my fingers in his ears, they got so hot."
(The mother...) "I think this will restore our home. This is going to bring a lot of happiness and things we have hoped for for a long, long time. Since the day he was born, I have prayed for a complete healing. And now I think we can be a complete family."

"Poor circulation, my right leg was shorter, my leg got stretched out...my pulse came back. I didn't have a pulse in either leg. I had a sore arm. It's all gone." (Man with a strong German accent.)

"I had scoliosis of the spine since second grade. They grew out my legs...my feet started tingling and I got healed." (Girl)

"Believers are praying for a lady in a wheelchair who had her leg cut off. The leg has already grown out three inches and they say the bone is forming in the leg."

"He came in on a walker. He couldn't bend his knees or nothing and they said he had a heart attack. The Lord gave him a new heart and he's walking...they haven't seen him walk in a year." (Old man)

(Mother) "My son is five-and-a-half years old and he's been deaf since birth. And he was healed tonight."

Jim from WCIE radio.., "We've been having such a good time ministering to people tonight. It's been so exciting to see people want God to move in their lives. I know that the Word works. God is not a man that He should lie. When the Bible says, praise God, that these signs shall follow the believer, He wasn't joking! I sat thirteen hours watching the video tapes on Saturday. It's so exciting that these signs are following the believers, including me...and it's not just the pastors and Charles and Frances."

Dr Owellen... "This is a woman who WAS in a wheelchair."

Woman... "My wheelchair is out in the hall some-where. I could walk short distances. I had M.S." (She had come all the way across the church.) "I feel hot."

The man who healed her was a financial planner. "We couldn't see any results until through a word of knowledge, we cast out the spirit of unforgiveness and the healing then started."

"Frances prayed for me in Orlando and it didn't work. So I went to one of the healing teams. They cast a demon out of me that was causing my lupus. It felt like the demon was just ripping me apart inside. Now, all the pain is gone!"

"I'm saved! I'm healed! I want to thank Laurie from North Dakota and Tom from St. Petersberg. They worked with me in the prayer room. I was slain out in the hall and didn't get my hearing completely. I wasn't satis-fied. I met my husband...he had been down into the prayer room. He had surgery last September...a complete hip replacement. I said, 'John, I want to see you walk.' I had sent him to the prayer room where they were praying for the lengthening of limbs. I watched him walk and it was such a beautiful walk, I said, 'I gotta have that!'

"I noticed the other night they prayed for my hands because they weren't exactly as they should be...and they grew out. I went down here...and said 'My hearing is not here. I don't know exactly what it is...I don't want this to look like I don't have faith, but I want whatever my hus-band got.' I went to the room and sat down in the chair. These two people worked with me and cast out some spi-rits. I was on the floor one minute and up in the chair the next. They cast out each one as it came. And glory to God, I got it all! My right ear is almost completely healed! I've got all your books and tapes to learn how to do this my-self...they also gave me a whole set of new organs. Praise God!" (Woman)

"Lung cancer was diagnosed last May. I've been tak-ing radiation and had radiation pain tonight. The cancer is gone and the pain is all gone now." (Man)

"I want to give Jesus the glory and honor. I didn't know I had one short arm and one short leg. I am a runner and I always had a lot of pain in my legs. One of the people out there prayed for me. I watched my leg grow out. I watched my arm grow out." (Young man)

"I just got my feet healed. I had flat feet and every day when I wake up I'm going to praise God that He's helped my arches. I got new arches. I always tripped." (Young boy)

"My left hip was higher than my right. Jesus healed me. They grew out my leg. I stood up and *fainted*." (Girl)

"I received a new heart tonight from the Lord Jesus Christ. I just want the whole world to know that I love Him. I had a heart valve prolapse...like a hole in my heart...a valve that doesn't work right. I was taking pills three times a day. I've been praying every day. I went two weeks without and the devil tempted me. I swallowed one pill. I felt bad. I took about one a week if I needed them. After tonight I won't be needing them at all. I feel differently now. I used to hang on every heart beat and live in fear. Now it's all gone." (Woman)
(Editor's note: Stay on medication until your doctor takes you off.)

"I have diabetes and heart failure. From time to time I have a severe headache...for about ten years. Tonight I have nothing...no headache...no pain. I am Egyptian. This lady can see now. Before that she can't see at all. Medically, she was blind. I am a medical doctor. I had a coronary and some medication. The doctor said to me if I have another attack, I must have open heart surgery. I am afraid and I came today for you to pray for me." (A doctor)

"Praise the name of Jesus. I am a medical doctor, too. I am his sister-in-law. I came today because I know that I have a small tumor in the ovary. I know that the power of God did a miraculous healing. Also, I have a short one leg. Incidentally, the power of the Lord grew a half inch of my foot. I'm going to lay hands on the sick and heal them."

The Reports Kept Coming
From The Lips Of Those Healed And
Those Who Did The Healing

Pat from Orlando: "God healed me and set me free. He set me free and did a whole new job. I had some problems with my heart...erratic heart beats. God just totally healed me. Praise God."

Earlene from Tampa: "I had heart disease, lung disease, arthritis, kidney trouble, diabetes...you name it...I got it, but Jesus took care of it tonight."

Barbara from Tarpon Springs, Florida: "My husband and I had contracted herpes before we were born again believers and we came here tonight to ask for joint healings. The Lord told me in September that I was to come tonight because He was going to heal us completely. I can still feel the precious anointing of Jesus all through my body at this time. We've been healed 100%. I know Jesus is alive more than I've ever felt in my life. It's just a fantastic feeling."

Clara: "I had this terrible pain in my neck and hip. The healing team began to pray and I felt it begin to move. I didn't know my foot was shorter than the other. I'm praising Jesus for my healing. I'm healed!"

Trudy from Lakeland: "I had scoliosis with always an ache. The Lord, His Spirit just slayed me. I don't have any pain at all now."

Lillian: "Many years ago I fell and slipped on my floor. I had two ribs that did not grow back. The doctor said they were broken off from the spine and rubbed a nerve. Nothing could be done since I was eighty years old. I met this gentleman yesterday at the restaurant. He gave me this little book about Jesus to read. I wasn't going to come until I read that book. The same man is here tonight...he prayed for my legs and I am healed."

Jim from Melbourne: "I was amazed to see some big fellows, ...the bigger they were the harder they fell under God's power. People were healed with ear problems and a fellow with an ankle problem was healed. My pastor will be amazed when I go back on Sunday and tell him what we have done. I'm writing a letter of thanks to Charles and Frances. It's a fantastic ministry and I pray God blesses them."

R.D. from Delray Beach, Florida: "I was at the beau-

tiful Lakeland Healing Explosion. What a Jesus! What a
Holy Spirit we have! What a service! The healing team
that ministered to me grew out my arms and a long-
standing severe backache was healed. I heard three very
loud cracks come from my back while he held my hands
and I've not had a backache since then. The Lord is so
good!"

Paul from Indiana Shores, St. Petersberg area: "One
young man came up with T.M.S. While I was praying, I
sensed that he had a problem down his back. We had
prayed for his jaw and then we prayed for his back. He
put his arms out and started hollering as he watched his
arms growing out. He came back awhile later and said, 'I
just got healed. My jaw isn't clicking for the first time in
two years. I can open and close it without a problem. I
didn't think anything was wrong with my back, but now
I can bend my back in a way I never could before.'"

Lorina from Coral Springs, Florida: "I'm going to be
in Jacksonville! I'm going to help!"
Karen from St. Petersberg: "I had scoliosis, lupus,
arthritis, diabetes, and allergies. I came in pain and now
I'm healed. I have no pain."

Elisa from Lakeland: "I saw my legs grow out. The
pain is gone!"

Healing Team Reports Keep Pouring In
Chuck from Agape Lighthouse in Jacksonville: "I'm
on fire for the Lord. He is healing left and right out here.
I prayed for this one woman sitting in a wheelchair. She
said she'd been prayed for already. I said, 'Well, what are
you doing still sitting in that wheelchair?'

"She said, 'I don't know.' I prayed for her and commanded her in the name of Jesus to get up and walk out of that wheelchair. She got up and walked out of that wheelchair!

"I said, 'Now, you give God the glory. Don't you be sitting back in that wheelchair and give Satan the glory. You stand up and walk out of this building giving God the glory.' I saw her a few minutes ago and she was still walking."

From a pastor: "I have never seen anything like this before...not like this. All my life, I knew Jesus could heal, but I just didn't know how. This is the first time we have ever known just exactly what to do. I'll never be the same again. I mean it. We have been pastors in the past and just didn't know really what to do."

Dave: "A girl about my age came out and her ankle was hurting. I commanded it to be healed and she started turning it. She said 'Oh, it feels fine now.' Then my dad touched her head and she fell under the Spirit and didn't know what hit her."

Al: "My wife really does the praying and I do the catching. The first lady came out with poor hearing, arthritis across the back of her shoulders and cancer. We laid hands on her and she went down. When she stood up, she could hear, her pain was gone and she said her cancer was gone. She had lumps on her groin and her neck...they were both gone."

Wood from Orlando: "We ministered to a woman in a wheelchair with polio. We grew out her legs and then she got out of the wheelchair. She got out several times and each time her legs were stronger. We adjusted her neck and she could hear out of her deaf right ear. Praise the Lord."

Lorie from Leonard, N.D.: "I came here because I wanted to learn to heal people in a simpler way. I saw Charles and Frances in North Dakota in March. I just felt something happen. We prayed and I got to come down here. I love it. I didn't come here to get healed...I didn't know I needed healing. but, I have an incurable skin disease caused by a defective liver. They prayed a new liver into me...and I got it!! Now I'm ministering healing to other people. One woman had a hearing problem, many surgeries, cirrhosis, a tumor, only one lung and a painful shoulder from arthritis. She got totally healed. Praise God!"

From Tampa: "I've just seen miracles all over this place. Legs growing out, hands growing out, different diseases healed. It was just fantastic. I've never seen what I've seen here tonight. I'm on fire!"

Roy from Clearwater, Florida: "We ministered to a lady who had a severe nervous problem. We spoke peace into her spirit. While we were laying hands on her we felt the special anointing come out of us. She started weeping and laughing at the same time as the healing power went into her.

"One man we ministered to had a cyst on his back. His neck got very hot, like it was burning up. God was healing him and in just a few minutes he was normal. I've heard about this ministry. I was so glad to find you all."

Jim and Donna from Tampa: "One had blurry eyes,

another had a bad back. Another had a knee problem and back problem. They were healed."

Joanie: "We prayed for a pastor and his church. One woman had cataracts and got her eyesight. Another had a bad back. Another needed a new heart...and received one.

"I've never done anything like this. What was so nice was my girls, they're eleven and fifteen years old. They were right there in front of people, healing them, too. It didn't matter if they were children or adults...they could just come up and lay hands on them and the Lord worked through them."

Wilma from Ft. Myers: "I prayed for a mother. We grew her legs out. She was very skeptical...and then all of a sudden she said, 'Yep, yep, yep.' She got so excited she jumped up and said, 'Will you pray for my boy?'

"I turned around and her twelve-year-old son was there with asthma. The Lord had delivered me from it. I just asked, 'Do you believe?'

"He said, 'Oh, yes!' I laid hands on him and he just went down with this big grin on his face. He got up and said, 'Thank you!' I've never seen anything like this before!"

Connie: "A woman got a new set of lungs tonight, a marriage was restored, a daughter received Jesus. I have laid hands on the sick before, but I haven't ministered a creative miracle before!"

Barbie from Ona, Florida: "We ministered to a girl

with lupus.My husband and I just knew that when we cast the spirit away it had to come out. The first thing we knew she was buckled over and gagging...the spirit came out and the pain left. Ten minutes later she came back. The pain had come back into her shoulder. I looked right at her and rebuked the spirit of doubt. The pain disappeared instantly.

"We laid hands on a black lady who had pain from cancer in her stomach and was totally deaf. I commanded the spirit of cancer to come out and laid hands on her ears. She could hear and the pain was gone. The Lord told my husband and me that our ministry would start after tonight. It's beautiful!"

Judith from Ona, Florida: "I just ministered to a lady who had tinnitus in her ears. It left in the name of Jesus. She told me it also released her lungs and cleared them up. I also laid hands on a lady who had sinus problems. She talked through her nose. I commanded those sinuses to clear up and drain out of there. She went 'sniff' and they were clear.

"I have laid hands on the sick before...I'm an ordained minister and I have learned an awful lot through these classes. I saw the twelve hours of video teaching and read the book. It's made me realize that there are a lot of ways to heal diseases that I wasn't aware of before...those to do with growing out your legs and arms."

Alex from Baltimore, Maryland (Alex and his wife, Barbara, were present at the first four Healing Explosions): "I was in the room where they were growing out legs. I ministered to more than thirty people...lots of arthritis, short legs and back pain...instantly healed.

"It's fantastic to see God moving and to hear all the

miracles but what's more exciting is to see the people that have never ministered to the sick...to see the excitement and joy on their faces. They can go back home and no matter who they are, they can touch others in the name of Jesus and change people's lives."

Hear the Reports from the Healing Teams:
A pastor called and said, "I went to the Lakeland Healing Explosion and saw things I never saw in my entire life. You people make it so simple that it's hard to believe, but I tried it, and it changed my life. I have ministered healing successfully to more people in the last two weeks than I have in my whole ministry, and I have ministered the baptism with the Holy Spirit successfully to more people in the last two weeks than all of my ministry put together. I always tried to do it the hard 'religious' way, but you saw the simplicity and are sharing it with the body of Christ. Praise God for your ministry."

From the Photographer
"I love your 'Waffle House' Miracle. I thought you would enjoy my 'Bob Evans Restaurant Miracle". God is so wonderful. While Kay and I were having lunch at Bob Evans in Lakeland, Florida, we started talking to the folks at the table next to us.

"I invited them to the Healing Explosion at The Carpenter's Home Church. The elderly couple (in their eighties) told me of how she fell forty years ago in England and broke two ribs that healed without being set, her hips were out of alignment, she had a short leg and a large bump on her upper back. I made her promise she would come to the Healing Explosion. She said she would try. I told her I would expect to see her there.

"Tuesday rolled around and I got caught up taking

pictures and forgot about this lady. God allowed me to walk right into her. I asked her if she had been healed yet, and she said no one had prayed with her yet. So, I handed the camera to one of your employees and proceeded to heal her. Can you imagine *over 9,000 people present and God brought me right to her!* He is so wonderful! I grew out her arms and legs, commanded her hips to go into place and commanded the large bump (size of a golf ball) to be healed and it *totally disappeared* when she started walking. Then she said, 'My legs are fine and I don't limp. My hips are in place and the pain is gone.' Her husband and daughter put their hands on her back and they said the big bump was gone! God is still a God of signs, wonders and miracles!"

Action on the Street

"We had an opportunity to put into practice what we had learned immediately upon return from the Victory Breakfast. We were just a few blocks from home when a young woman ran into the side of our car on her bicycle. She got up from the road crying and claiming that her finger was broken. Jane bound Satan in the name of Jesus and commanded that the finger not be broken and that all pain must leave immediately. We remained with her for about five minutes to be sure she was O.K. and then prepared to leave. She thanked us for our concern and when she turned to leave, she shook hands with me *with the hand of the wounded finger.* When she realized what she had done, she was dumbfounded, and said, 'It doesn't even hurt.'

"Since that time Jane has personally administered healing to people with scoliosis, arthritis, high blood pressure, bad lungs, painful hips and shoulders, and aching backs. In all, over a dozen healings have taken place *in her dress shop!*

"I have been counseling with her (we're a team) with people with marital problems, drug and alcohol difficulties, grief, fear, unforgiveness, etc. as well as supervising the *construction* of our ministry."

Some Turn into Fanatics

"I praise the name of Jesus for your obedience to go forth and teach on how to heal the sick the way Jesus did. My family has not been the same and neither has my fellowship since November 5th, 1985. When you prayed, I received every anointing you both have plus the manifestation of all the gifts of the Spirit.

"Here are some of the things that happened November 5th at the Healing Explosion: A woman with spurs on heels had pain - it left in Jesus' name and spurs dissolved. A young lady (fifteen years old) in a wheelchair with cerebral palsy — couldn't feel from the waist down. Bound Satan and grew out legs, had her stand up which she did with the wheelchair as a prop. She began to cry because she had feeling in her legs for the first time.

"Another man had pain in his hips. The Lord showed me after I adjusted his legs that it was arthritis of his hip joints. I bound Satan and commanded the spirit of arthritis to leave and the pain went. It is now two weeks later and all the pain is gone and he is walking perfectly!

"November 6, 1985: A lady was healed instantly of a sore throat. The pain was gone! Then I adjusted the back of another woman and the pain disappeared.

"November 7, 1985: In my veterinarian clinic, a lady's left eye had a cataract. She had no vision except faint light. She was rigid with fear. I bound Satan, rebuked fear, laid hands on her eye and commanded the cataract to dissolve and spoke restoration. Within ten seconds she said the room brightened and then she could read fine print without glasses. She has been in three more times. The second time she received the baptism with the Holy Spirit.

"I could go on and on but last night our fellowship went with our musicians and singers and three people who were on healing teams. We *went at it* for Jesus and saw the following:

1. Bowed legs straightened out before our eyes!
2. Hereditary bent fingers straightened out immediately.
3. Two peoples' deaf ears opened.
4. A multitude of people with pain left healed.
5. Seven people were filled with the Holy Spirit.

                                    With Love, Ralph

P.S. My three-and-one-half year old son was having a problem with bedwetting. I adjusted his back, legs, arms and neck and he has not wet the bed since November 6, 1985. Praise God!"

Persistence Pays Off

"No words can express my joy and excitement in participating as a member of the healing team at The Carpenter's Home Church, November 5, 1985. As I received the anointing, my joy and excitement nearly burst my chest. When I heard the command, 'Sic 'em', I was ready. I was walking, but I wanted to run up the aisle. I was ready to tackle anything. I was ready to get any devil that had come in that place in a person's body.

"But when the first person came to my partner and me, my faith went right out the bottom of my feet. My heart fell like the walls of Jericho. The man was 82 or 92 (I don't remember which). He was helped along with the aid of his two granddaughters. His body was bent with paralysis or arthritis. His hands were stiff with no movement at all.

"My mind went blank and with that my faith also left. I KNEW I could not do anything for him. I had left Christ out of my purpose for being there. I write this with a great deal of pain, sorrow and tears, but I sent him away with his two granddaughters to have his legs grown out.

"Praise the Lord, at the breakfast the next morning testimony was given that he was healed!"
(Special note: This man testified on the stage of his healing!)

"Feeling that my anointing had surely left me, I decided I had to try again. I prayed for something easy, but since the Lord is smarter than I am, He sent me a woman with no hearing in her left ear and brainstem damage. I was not clear as to her symptoms because my mind was still on the man I had sent away.

"I heard my partner casting out demons and realized the woman was rocking between my partner and me. The woman said something and I looked at her face. She was crying and saying that her hearing had returned and the symptoms of brainstem damage were gone. I told my partner, 'That was easy, bring on some more.'

"I thank Jesus for your teaching. Certainly my life will never be the same. I still have thoughts of 'What if I can't...' and knowing full well it is Satan putting that in my mind. I feel all healing partners should see one another periodically to stay charged, sort of like charging a battery."

And They Healed Them All
"I just want to express my appreciation for your

ministry and for coming to Lakeland for the Healing Explosion.

"I know my life will never be the same. I had the privilege of being on the healing team and it was one of the greatest things I have ever experienced in my life.

"My wife and I saw many healings manifested as we ministered to the people. *The next night after the explosion our pastor let the healing teams minister to the sick. Everyone to whom we ministered testified that they had gotten healed!*

"We are so excited because now we can show people a living Christ with evidence they can't deny. We know this is going to open many doors to lead people to Jesus and into the baptism."

I Watched A Tumor Disappear

"My first 'patient' was a man who came staggering out the door. I asked what his problem was. TERMINAL CANCER! (God, couldn't you start me on a sore toe?) Well, I FELT THE BOLDNESS OF A TIGER! I did everything you taught us to do. As my hand was on his right upper chest, I could feel that thing squirming around. I then put my hands on his cheeks and said, 'Brother, you're healed!'

"He said, 'I BELIEVE IT!'

"Then there was a lady with a long list of things written down...high blood pressure, diabetes, vision loss, bad hearing, bad back. I ministered *as taught* to each disease and commanded the spirit to go. She fell under the power. I knelt down and put my hand where her new pancreas was jumping around! *I believe I was actually feeling spiritual surgery as it was being performed! THANK YOU, JESUS!*

"A young woman came to me. She had a knot under

arm and several in her breast. I ministered as you taught and told her to try to find it, and she said, 'It's gone!' Wow! Praise Jesus! Also tapped a wrist and *watched* a tumor disappear!

"In the prayer room at church today I ministered to a lady with scoliosis, glaucoma, sore neck and back, short leg and short arm. She fell under the power of God. Then to top it off, a first-time visitor accepted forgiveness from Jesus, received the baptism with the Holy Spirit and was also delivered."

Revival Started At Lakeland Healing Explosion
"I have never been so excited in my whole life! Never would I have dreamed about being on a healing team!! Ever since I was a child being raised in a Southern Baptist Church, I knew way down in my heart God could do anything. But I never dreamed He'd use me! Hallelujah!

"I could write a book about the things that have happened during and after the Healing Explosion in Lakeland. I teach at a Christian school and I've never had more fun in my life. We've cast out the spirit of asthma, commanded headaches to go, grown legs and arms out and on and on.

"We have been fasting and praying for revival since school began. *And is it exciting to see God work!*"

Aftermath of the Explosion
FROM EATON PARK, FL.: "I am so excited, I hardly can sleep at night because I was in the audience at the Healing Explosion in Lakeland, Florida. The Lord kept telling me to go there since I first heard about it a few months ago. When the night came, I was very depressed and doubtful. (My husband is a 'lukewarm Christian' and certainly skeptical about 'faith healing'. We are

Lutherans.)

"I cranked up my courage and went that night after trying to talk my husband into it, too...but of course, he wouldn't go. I was happy to be there and as I felt more at ease (the worshipping is totally different than Lutheran's), I felt as if I wanted to believe every bit of it.

"When it came to the healing part, you kept saying, 'Healing is yours. Come and claim it in Jesus' name and don't let anyone take your healing afterward.' I was shy and so reserved as I approached one on the healing team. My back has been a terrible problem to me for many years. I have been going to a chiropractor for years and it is a well known fact my left leg was 1/2 inch or more shorter than the right (thus the major problem causing all the rest).

"That night it actually grew when the healing team people prayed for me. I couldn't believe it was really happening to me and sort of went home in a daze. No one I have showed it to denies that the feet are straight and one is not shorter than the other. I have been looking in the mirror for three days now...I guess I keep expecting to see that left leg shorter than the other. Like it wouldn't last...but I praise Him all the time. The most wonderful thing to me is to find out His miracles can happen to ANYONE. I am just a plain average wife and mother who only about one-and-one-half years ago became a born again Christian. I have been witnessing to anyone that will listen to my story.

"Tell people these are miracles that do happen in 1985 and happen to 'plain folks' not just certain people. Praise the Lord for the wonderful things He does!" J.N.

It Didn't Stop At Lakeland!
"Praise the Lord for you two! I was never so blessed

and enriched as during the 'Healing Explosion' in Lakeland, Florida. Jim and I were amazed, dumbfounded and awed by God's miracle working power. For the first time in twelve months or more the urging and frustration that I felt was eased. I felt that finally I could do something for my Lord Who had done so much for me. I can never tell you the love, appreciation and admiration I have for you. My faith is truly high and I am excited about doing the same 'works that Jesus did' in my own church and hometown and wherever the Lord sends me.

"I want to share with you a dream or vision that I had on Friday morning, November 8th, after the 'Healing Explosion'. We had pulled our camper to Florida to attend your seminar; and about five or five thirty a.m., I awoke and was going to reach out and pick up the alarm clock to see what time it really was. But I couldn't move or open my eyes. I knew it was lighter outside.

"About that time I saw myself in a strange city at the bottom of some stairs and it was on a city street somewhere and I was ministering to a pregnant lady as we were standing on the bottom of the steps. I could even feel the unborn child moving under my hands as I placed my hands on her stomach.

"Then I heard a number of voices shouting, 'Jesus is coming, Jesus is coming.' I ran up the steps and was standing on a street in a city with sky-scrapers and saw all the people in the streets and on the sidewalks and I finally lifted my eyes to the skies and I saw Jesus. He was so big. I remember thinking that the Bible said every eye shall see Him, and I knew that there was no way that everyone could not see Him. His head was at the heavens, or sky. His arms were outstretched and His body seemed to flow toward the earth but not on it. I knew it was Jesus and as I looked up, I remember saying to myself, "Lord, surely, I'm not going to be left." About that time He seemed to say, 'Arise, arise', and I felt my feet leave the ground and the dream or vision ended.

"Needless to say, after the 'Healing Explosion' and being privileged to be on a healing team, I was awed and I wanted to beat my husband, Jim, on the shoulder to say, 'Look, look,' but I couldn't move. I felt like I saw the rapture and I remember thinking this is just like the Bible says, we will be doing our regular thing or jobs when He appears. Praise the Lord! (I'm still so excited.)

"I have never experienced anything like this in my life and I wanted to share it with you because I believe it happened because of the faith in the 'Healing Explosion' and the healing that I was a part of. I *knew* it was from God.

"Also, I would like to share that in December of 1983, Jim, my husband, had a massive heart attack at age sixty and was defibrillated (I couldn't find the word in the dictionary) twenty-seven times. As you know this is medical history. God at that time gave me the 'gift of faith'. It's a long story, but God moved and I talked with the Holy Spirit, spoke with an angel and saw angels and fought demons. Praise the Lord.

"In December of 1984, Satan attacked Jim again...this time with a lump under his left arm. It started like a small pebble and in about two weeks it was like a biscuit. It was removed and we were told he had cancer. Needless to say, we went to God and the Word and God gave us such assurance. And on December 31, 1984, after many tests, x-rays, etc., the doctors can't find any trace of cancer and still do not understand. Praise the Lord. (And on December 11, 1985, we went back for more tests, x-rays, blood work etc. Still no cancer.) God is so good. We know God is in the healing business. And now you can understand why I want to do something for my Lord who has done so much for me.

"On Sunday, November 12th after Sunday School, we ministered to several members of our Sunday School class. Jim grew out a man's arm and legs and he then could move his arms and touch his back. He couldn't put on his coat without help before. Another man lived with pain in his chest from an old football injury and said the doctor told him he had arthritis at the site of the injury. He said it was like spasms around the heart and very painful. I bound the devil and cast out the spirit of arthritis and he went out under the power of God's Holy Spirit. He got up healed and completely free of pain...and still is.

"We shared with our pastor (Methodist Church) on the following Friday morning and he sanctioned all that we were doing and told us to keep it up. Praise the Lord. After that meeting we met our daughter and two-and-a-half-year-old grandson at McDonald's and saw the man that had been healed of arthritis with a local attorney. I went over later to speak to Joel and the attorney asked me point blank if I would heal his shoulder. Joel had been sharing with him what happened to him on Sunday. Praise God, He heals arthritis in McDonald's. The attorney could reach his arm over his head and all pain was gone.

"Thank you for opening a door for us and making our lives more exciting. I can hardly wait for each day. Praise the Lord!

"In Jesus' name,"   Merle

"Not By Might, Nor By Power,
But By My Spirit, Saith The Lord"
"The first week of November Charles and Frances

Hunter had a Healing Explosion in Lakeland. The morning of the breakfast Karen Wheaton began singing "Touch Thru Me Holy Spirit". The power of God fell on people all over the auditorium. I began crying and just felt the presence of the Lord. It was a beautiful morning, in fact, the entire Healing Explosion was full of miracles and the presence of God. I knew something had happened to me that week. I didn't know what, I just knew I was a different person. I had an excitement in my spirit. In fact, the week after the meeting, I remember I was so happy and full of joy, David and I put the Christmas tree up.

"In December I discovered I was pregnant! Yes, that is a *miracle*. David and I will be married seven years in February and haven't had a baby. But there had been another miracle. I hadn't wanted any children; and when I knew I was pregnant I was so happy and full of joy. God had changed my heart from a selfish wife to a giving wife! I used to say the rapture is coming. Jesus could be here by 1988. Why should I bring a baby into this wicked world? Why should I go through the "trouble" and "pain" of childbirth when I will be leaving this planet to go home to heaven in a few years? Why shouldn't I concentrate on a ministry, concentrate on getting people that are already here saved and right with God.

"Well, my thinking changed. I was a totally different person when I realized something very important. When a baby is born into this world, it is no accident. The couple who had sex may have said it was an accident, but it was no accident with God. Every baby has a purpose. Babies born in over-populated areas of the world have a purpose. Babies born in countries with famine have a purpose. Babies born in oppressed countries have a purpose. God has a purpose for everything He does.

"One night God let me have a wonderful experience. I saw a mother with a baby in a poverty area. I focused on the baby. I know life does not come from Satan. Satan kills. God gives life. As I focused on the baby, I got such a warm, peaceful feeling. I saw life...a precious spirit. I saw the baby as being special and alive — not as "flesh and blood and another mouth to feed".

"When God gives life it is special, it has a purpose. Each individual has meaning. God does not do anything without purpose. As I thought about this I got so blessed and so full of love for my *miracle* that God had given David and me. I have told God I will do all I physically can for this special life. I will care for and protect this life and do all I know to make this baby a healthy child; and I have given this baby to God. This baby isn't mine. This baby is a miracle. God has a purpose for this baby.

"About a week before the doctor had confirmed my pregnancy, I was talking to a special friend. We were talking about her family and she said, 'Nancy, somebody I know is going to have a boy. I don't know who it is, I just know it. Oh, well,' and we continued our conversation.

"A couple of days later I was driving home from the store and a thought came into my mind, 'I'm going to name him Lucas.' I even said it out loud, 'Lucas! I don't even know anybody by that name, or even if it is a first name.' So I smiled and said, 'We'll call him Luke — after the third book in the New Testament.'

"After David and I had confirmed we were parents by the doctor's tests, we were looking at names for babies. In the book 'Lucas' was listed. It means 'Light'. I thought, 'How appropriate.' David's and my *miracle* is named 'Light'. God has a very special purpose for Lucas. I believe it with all my heart.

"Isn't it something how God can change a person's

life? I wonder how many people God 'touches' at different services and they and others don't even realize it. We can see a physical healing, like a person being healed and able to get out of a wheelchair, or when a person is healed and is able to remove a brace; and we can see when God's power comes upon a person and they begin crying, or get filled with joy, and give a testimony of being healed of a headache, or a tumor leaving, or sores drying up; but how about people like me who just start crying during the meeting, not knowing why, leaving the meeting and just knowing 'something's different'. I can't tell you what, I just know something's different.

"God blesses people all the time and we don't SEE it. God isn't limited to just physical healings. God is a God of miracles. God is able to heal mental and spiritual afflictions also. We really should be a people of PRAISE and THANKSGIVING."

Nancy

Victory Breakfast

The Victory Breakfast the next morning was attended by over 1,000 ecstatic members of the healing teams who the night before discovered the amazing wonders of seeing God's healing power flow through "even them".

For over an hour they lined up to excitedly tell of the marvels that had happened at the Lakeland Healing Explosion! They were limited to telling only one or two miracles but the volume of healings reported was reminiscent of what happened through Jesus while He was on the earth; "And I suppose that if all the other events in Jesus' life were written, the whole world could hardly contain the books!" (John 21:25 TLB).

Pastor Karl Strader who has ministered in Pentecost

for many years and has had all of the well-known ministries of healing in his church over the years, said of the Lakeland Healing Explosion, "In all my years of Pentecost, I've never seen anything like this!"

Did God repeat what He had done at Pittsburgh? He even outdid Himself! Letters continue to arrive daily telling us of the wondrous and mighty acts of God done that wonderful night at the Carpenter's Home church.

Chapter Twelve

The Foothills of the Denver Healing Explosion

God can make a miracle out of anything and everything! The first night of training for the Denver Healing Explosion was a surprise because we had not anticipated such a crowd, and did not have room for everyone at the hotel meeting place, so we had to turn between two and three hundred people away. God is moving on the entire body of Christ to begin to do the same things that Jesus did! It was beautiful, however, to see no bad attitudes as people were turned away and instructed to go to the Coliseum the next day.

We had found it necessary to change the meeting place just two weeks before the meeting and did our best to get the public notified. This could have caused a big problem, but all it did was to hurt the attendance slightly, but not the spirit!

Miracles happened even before the service started. A man was healed of a chronic back problem which had him in pain for years. A woman was healed just standing on the stage, waiting to be touched! A woman with a body totally crippled with arthritis was literally encompassed by the Spirit of God and every single bit of the arthritis left and she really danced a jig because of the extreme joy and excitement. We could tell from the very first moment that the Denver healing teams were going to be something special! The microphones were not hooked up yet, but you couldn't stop them from singing.

Cold weather had set in, but it didn't dampen or cool the spirits of those who had come to be obedient to Jesus and do the things He has commanded us to do.

Chartered buses became a necessity to transport the people to the Coliseum, food service became a problem to everyone because of inadequate facilities, but God overcame in all circumstances and all the sessions brought one of the most excited group of people attending training sessions that we had ever seen. They were so wild they could have successfully had a Healing Explosion the first night without any additional training!

Healings occurred throughout all of the training classes, and again the students were thrilled with the doctors' panel which included a dentist who gave some outstanding help in healing teeth.

God had begun moving on children before the date of the Healing Explosion. One young man attended one of our meetings in Boulder and wrote the following note:

"I was at your meeting the twenty-first and it was my third year anniversary of being born again! Well, that night in Boulder I was filled with the Spirit and received my prayer language!

"During the offering God told me to give $100, so here it is! I am believing God for a hundred-fold return.

"I have decided to be a member of a healing team in the upcoming Healing Explosion in Denver!
Love in Jesus,

Brenton
P.S. I forgot to tell you, *I am ten years old.* I will write
      you when I get my hundred-fold return. "

The Victory Processional group from Lincoln, Nebraska, consisting of three adults and approximately
twenty-five children between the ages of six and twelve,
thrilled the entire audience as they came down the aisle
singing "We Proclaim the Name of the Lord!" The audience had been singing for about an hour prior to the
meeting and was ready to be blessed by this Spirit-filled
group. All of the children in the group had studied the
book, watched the video tapes and had done all the
things that were necessary to qualify to be on the healing
teams.

When the actual "Healing Explosion" started and
the audience came down onto the floor for healing, the
children worked in teams of from two to five. What a
beautiful sight to see children with no doubt and unbe-
lief walk to a wheelchair, minister to the individual and
then command them to "get up and walk in the name of
Jesus!" We were on the stage letting people testify of
healings when five children, the oldest no more than
nine, brought an old lady who was suffering from arthritis. They had commanded the foul spirit to come out
and out it came! She was now walking up the stairs and
across the stage. The children were so thrilled, they could
hardly wait to get back to the next wheelchair.

They tackled the second one with the same zeal and
faith they had for the first, and to everyone's astonish-
ment, the second person came out of the wheelchair.
They expected results, and they got results!

When the service was over, these same children came
up to us in the back of the auditorium and told us that a

third woman had gotten up out of a wheelchair later on in the evening, but then she just sat back down again. They told us they "commanded the spirit of stubbornness to come out of her!" Glory, would that we all had the faith of little children!

Children of all ages were ministering healing right along with the adults and seeing spectacular results.

Confirmation In Denver

A word from the Lord came in Denver concerning the Healing Explosions. God spoke through a pastor and said, *"A nation-wide Healing Explosion will be first, but be ready, yes, I say, be ready for the day is fast approaching when there will be a world-wide satellite program when those you have trained to heal the sick will minister around the world through this means as you direct from a central location, and the WORLD WILL BE HEALED IN ONE NIGHT!"*

This seemed so impossible to us we felt there was no way that it could possibly happen, but something occurred in Denver that made us wonder if this is truly what God is preparing for this day and time.

Denver brought this into focus because there were representatives from twelve foreign countries who came to take the message back to their own countries..."*PEOPLE HEALING PEOPLE*". They came from Korea, Japan, Turkey, Pakistan, India, Colombia, Canada, Venezuela, Libya, Philippines, Poland and France! The Lakeland Explosion had representatives from Canada, Puerto Rico and Jamaica. Pittsburgh's great July 4th Explosion was visited by those from Canada, Germany and Ireland. God is supernaturally moving by His Spirit ALL OVER THE WORLD to prepare His people, His army of believers! Get ready!

Two prophetic words — one in Lakeland and one in Denver — have caused us to speed up our efforts to get the entire body of Christ ready for the supernatural move of God by training multitudes to heal the sick. A senator from Oklahoma called saying, "I've got to have a set of those healing tapes!" God is supernaturally moving on all flesh, encouraging them to sharpen up the tools which He has already given us so we can put in the sickle and reap the harvest. Healing is a tool which God gives... Jesus said, "If you don't believe me because of the words I say, then believe me because of the miracles you see me do!"

We feel an urgency in our spirits more than ever before to see the body of Christ in action, fully trained in healing. We have never seen such a hunger, and in just three explosions, we have seen more than 4,000 people receive training. Whenever a video school of healing opens in your area, be sure to attend!

When the power of God moves mightily, people have visions and many receive a word from the Lord. Here is one that especially touched us from a pastor's wife who attended the Denver Healing Explosion:

"The Lord moved in so many wonderful ways, but the most glorious thing I saw that night was during praise and worship. I had a beautiful vision. *We were singing 'All Hail, King Jesus' and I saw Jesus as king! It was the most beautiful sight I have ever beheld. Jesus was sitting on a golden throne which was seated on a white marble pedestal. He was wearing a red velvet robe with a gold belt and a gold and jeweled inlaid pendant. His cape was pure white fur, but not animal fur. He also had a gold and jeweled inlaid scepter.*

"His arms were spread out blessing us. Then He knelt down to us, His servants. It brought tears to my

eyes. The love He displayed was so strong and yet so gentle. Then I saw Him walking to His Father with His bride on His arm, and it became clear to my spirit that all of us there that night were in one accord and we represented the bride for which Jesus is coming back...every foreign country and every church and denomination acting in one accord. Now I know the kind of bride Jesus desires. I'll never forget this vision. It was more beautiful than words can describe."

Another vision was given to an eleven-year-old boy during praise on November 22, 1985 at the Denver Healing Explosion:

"There was a red man and a white man and they both had swords. The area looked like a desert and the ground was all cracked and dry. There were desert type trees.

"When they fought, their swords touched and the swords would spark liquid gold which changed to water on the parched ground. The red man's sword disappeared and the man grew larger and larger until he was four times bigger than the white man.

"Then the white man's sword turned into a Bible. The white man opened it and he grew to the same size as the red man. He pulled out the helmet of salvation and the breastplate of righteousness. He girded his loins and shod his feet. He put on the whole armor of God and took up the shield of faith.

"His Bible became a sword again and he made a triangular shaped cut into the red man and then stabbed in the center of the triangle. The red man broke into millions of little red demons and then the white man separated into millions of glowing white humans. The demons ran as fast as they could but the people walked after them and destroyed them all."

Chapter Thirteen

God Showered His Blessings

In Denver

"Then David went into the Tabernacle and sat before the Lord and prayed, 'O Lord God, why have you showered your blessings on such an insignificant person as I am? And now, in addition to everything else, you speak of giving me an eternal dynasty! Such generosity is far beyond any human standard! Oh, Lord God! What can I say? For you know what I am like! You are doing all these things just because you promised to and because you want to! How great you are, Lord God! We have never heard of any other god like you. And there is no other god'" (2 Samuel 7:18-22 TLB).

Perhaps in our fear of being prideful, or perhaps because our faith has been covered with the dust of false modesty, the body of Christ has shrunk back into a position of insignificance in the work assigned to us by our Lord and Savior Jesus Christ. Who are we to believe we can, as ordinary believers, assume the role of rulers today over the powers of darkness in this world?

Shouldn't we wait until after we return to earth from heaven?

Did Jesus Speak the Truth?

by Frances

"Most assuredly, I say to you, he who believes in Me, the works that I do he will do also; and greater works than these he will do, because I go to My Father" (John 14:12 NKJV).

That verse always fascinates both of us because we love the supernatural, and we love to operate in the supernatural, but did Jesus actually mean that you and I could do exactly the same things He did? He must have, or He would not have said it in the Bible. Does He actually expect us to go out and do not only the same things that He did, but even greater ones? He must have, or He would not have made that statement!

I have studied that over and over, but recently I decided to go back and read it totally in context before and after the scripture appears, and God gave me a fascinating revelation which I'll share with you.

Following that scripture two verses appear which are wonderful prayer scriptures. "And whatever you ask in My name, that I will do, that the Father may be glorified in the Son. If you ask anything in My name, I will do it." Did He actually say that would apply in everyday life, or was it to be applied under certain circumstances? We all like to believe that we can ask anything in His name and He will do it, but look when and where He makes that promise: He says if we're out there doing the same things that He did, and even greater things than He did, *then* we can ask for anything, and He will do it for us because we are doing what He told us to do.

The day I received that revelation I nearly exploded at the seams. Never again do you have to stand in front of a "hopeless" cripple and wonder where the power is going to come from to heal that individual. Jesus said that when you were being obedient to Him by doing His works, you could ask for anything (not for your own glory, but that the Father might be glorified in the Son) and could expect an answer. He didn't tell us to ask *Him* to do greater miracles than He did when He was on earth, He told us to go and do them ourselves.

The interesting thing is that He didn't tell us we could ask Him for anything and would know it was done if we were asking for our sore toe, or possibly a healing in our marriage, or possibly a healing in our finances, but He said when we were out doing His works, that is the time when we could ask for anything and would know that it would be done! Glory!

by Charles and Frances

Today is the day of salvation! Today, right here on this earth, we are to take the full authority given to us by Jesus, the full responsibility He placed squarely upon our shoulders to present the gospel with mighty signs and wonders so people will see Jesus alive in us today! The body of Christ has been a sleeping giant, so why shouldn't the sinful people of the world, or even Christians, see Jesus either dead, asleep, or waiting in heaven for His day to come, because they have been doing nothing to convince the world otherwise!

The body of Christ is now awakening to the realization that Jesus intends for us to take dominion over the demonic powers and sicknesses which we allow to dominate the people of this earth, right in front of our noses.

The third major Healing Explosion was in Denver, Colorado, and what an awesome demonstration of the rulership over sickness and demonic powers we saw as believers boldly stepped forth in the Denver Coliseum and took possession of this kingdom of God on earth!

These believers, just as in Pittsburgh and Lakeland, had been trained thoroughly by studying the book "To Heal the Sick", watching twelve hours of video tapes prepared by us, and then attending the training sessions and doctors' panel. They were as charged as electricity when that night arrived for them to move into the arena for action!

Let them tell you what happened as they share testimonies of the wonders of God's healing power through them, the "insignificant ones" like King David! When God and Christ Jesus live in us, we know we have been chosen for a work now on earth, and even to have an eternal home in heaven. But first, we must be servants of the Most High God to prepare others for that great day when we will enter into His heavenly glory!

We pray that you will inhale the exciting changes taking place in these believers as they share this new world of healing and delivering power vested in them by our Lord Jesus.

(Note: In some of the testimonies following, you will see where they mention standing on the carpet. We had four rows of twelve-foot wide carpet on the two hundred foot long floor of the Coliseum for the convenience of people falling under the power of the Holy Spirit.)

Grant Your Servants Great Boldness
"Dear Charles and Frances,

"Thank you so much for being obedient to our Heavenly Father, Almighty God, and coming to Denver to hold a Healing Explosion. Thank you for being so humble that you would spend your precious time teaching us, the laymen, how to do the works for Jesus and to heal the sick. Through this teaching the zeal of God has been fanned into a roaring fire again within me. We appreciate you and praise God for you, His ministry gift to us.

by Dianne:

"As the Healing Explosion teaching sessions progressed, I became more and more excited about the mighty works God was about to do. It is awesome to be a vessel for the Holy Spirit and to watch what He will do through a totally yielded vessel. I thank my Lord and Savior for the privilege to be used by Him to minister to a sick, lost and dying world.

"Friday night before the start of the Healing Explosion and before praise and worship began, I left the floor of the Coliseum for a little while. When I returned to the floor, the compassion of Jesus was so strong that I wept as I entered into the area...wept for the sick, the crippled, the blind, the lame, those bound by Satan. The whole floor was charged with the anointing and the expectations of the saints. You could feel the presence of God even before praise and worship began. I remember wondering during praise and worship whether any of us would be able to stand up to minister since the presence of God was so strong. But God is faithful and He equips those He calls and we were able to stand in His presence and minister His healing.

"At first my husband was the 'catcher' and I was ministering but as we progressed we alternated as we had direction from the Lord, sometimes both ministering to the same person in shifts. I am very petite and didn't think I could catch anyone bigger than children. God is faithful and I never had to catch anyone, they only fell when my husband was there to catch them. Praise the Lord!

"The first lady to whom we ministered had a kneecap which had been removed surgically and her other one needed surgery. She could hardly bend her legs. She also had fibrocystic disease in her breasts and wanted to be delivered from cigarettes. We took care of the cigarettes first by binding the spirit behind the smoking and releasing her from the addiction to nicotine. Then we had her repeat a prayer renouncing cigarettes and proclaiming that she would no longer pollute the temple of the Holy Spirit (she was Spirit-filled) while she crushed the cigarettes under her feet.

"I spoke new knee caps into both of her legs and restoration of all muscles, ligaments, tendons and associated tissues. I bound the spirit behind the fibrocystic disease and cast it out, commanded the lumps to be gone and spoke healthy tissue to replace it. Then I touched her forehead lightly and said, "Lord, bless her" and she fell under the power of God. This is the first time God used me in that way and I was so excited! She got up and was able to do deep knee bends, something she could not do before. And when she pressed on her breasts she could not feel the lumps! Praise Jesus!

"I'll let my husband, Joseph, tell the rest of the praise reports.

by Joseph:

"I praise my Father God for the greatest healing which took place on the Coliseum floor — mine! My wife is a great blessing from God and I have always believed in and loved Jesus. I was born again and Spirit-filled but

I was not a witness for my Lord. I kept my mouth shut and pretended everything was O.K. I was asleep in the world and walking the defeated Christian walk.

"I want to thank you for your faithfulness to come and teach us to be the followers of Jesus He wants us to be. I always wanted more than I was, but was afraid to ask or try. I almost didn't come. But God has given me a wife worth more than all the gold God created. She lovingly asked me to join her to go to the session you had at Good Shepherd Christian Center in Boulder. God did the rest. I knew that night that I had to attend your Healing Explosion and once and for all time either step up or sit down.

"I listened and learned and stepped out on the Coliseum floor in faith. I wanted to be proven by God. He DID! He set my hands on fire — a fire felt by others even when they had their backs turned and did not know that I was extending my hands toward them. They felt the fire of the Holy Spirit. Praise the Lord! I asked God for one thing on that floor — boldness to forever hold up the Lord Jesus to the world.

"The next person God brought to us to minister to was a young boy. He told us that he was legally blind in one eye. He could not see anything beyond six feet and then it was blurred and like shadows. We asked how long he had been like this and discovered that not only was he stricken with blindness but also his mother and brothers. We bound Satan in the name of Jesus and also the spirit of heredity. Then we spoke to the eye, the blood, the brain and the nerves to be healed in the name of Jesus. We asked him what he could see. He told us that the clock at the top of the Coliseum said, "Coca-Cola" and that he could read the numbers. Praise You, Jesus!

"I wore the red healing ribbon to work the following

week. I was greeted with silent stares, uncomfortably ventured jests, and some uncomfortable questions. They were uncomfortable, but not me. God made me bold! I answered according to the Word. I shared Jesus and His healing power and His love. Most wanted to get away from me, however, I know seed has been sown for Jesus. Two ladies were healed. Both had pain in their lower back. I grew out their legs and arms and spoke in the name of Jesus for the pain to be gone. Praise the Lord! One lady had been hobbling all day and was shocked when Jesus healed her! The other woman was very quiet and very watchful of me afterwards when her pain left her body instantly.

"Praise the Lord. I know I will do more. I know God is going to bring all of those people at work, at home, in my church to the same place He has brought me.

"God bless you both. We share your vision and God is helping us minister to our brothers and sisters. Tonight is Thanksgiving. We invited people from our church and home fellowship group to our home. After praising the Lord and eating, we praised the Lord again. We had everyone share something for which they were thankful. We were thankful for what God did for us at your Healing Explosion.

"We then asked for anyone wanting to be healed to raise their hand. Out of thirty present only a couple raised their hands. So we had them all stand and stretch out their arms. Praise the Lord! Better than half a dozen had noticeable differences. We started ministering just the way you showed us. Soon they were seeing and experiencing the healing power of God. Praise You, Jesus! We then asked if anyone of them would like to do the ministering. Before it was over, we had six other people ministering healing to others. God was glorified and the level of faith was exploding within many.

"The body of Christ is rising up out of the earth and shall soon shine like stars in the sky to the world.

"God bless you both abundantly!"

Love,
Diane and Joseph

Friday Night Happened So Fast

FROM COLORADO SPRINGS: "Wasn't it tremendous? Isn't it spectacular? Won't it be marvelous? Hundreds and thousands of believers setting the world on fire for God.

"Well, we had a wonderful time and were a great healing team. The Lord made us as one in the Spirit. We just couldn't wait for Friday night, so right after we got our ribbons we laid hands on a lady who had severe back problems and was selling her horses. But God gave her a miracle. She went out under the power of God, was healed and was so excited that she would be able to go horseback riding again.

"Also that day, my partner laid hands on a friend who had arthritis in the knees and delivered him from pain and stiffness.

"That Friday night happened so fast. We ran out of sick people to minister to in no time. We could have gone on for hours.

"After we prayed for a baby, the parents were so excited and even though the mother wasn't going to ask for prayer, she changed her mind. She had had surgery (a caesarean section and hysterectomy) and had scars and pain. I hardly got past, 'In Jesus' name', AND SHE WENT OUT IN THE POWER OF GOD and was healed. Saw her the next day and she said all scars were gone and all pain was gone. The husband went under the power of

God and was healed of many inner hurts and pains.
"WE WANT MORE!!"

"I Am A Part Of The End-time Harvest!"

"I'm the one with the back trouble and who is pigeon-toed. NO MORE! Thank You, Jesus! My feet
worked and moved all the way home. Then my knee
worked, then the healing touched my left hip and then
went over to the other hip. The next day I wasn't bow-
legged any more either...first night I ever slept without
hurting to get up the next morning. Praise God.

"I was at every class of the Healing Explosion in
Denver. I sure have learned a lot. Thank You, Jesus, it
works!

"At the Healing Explosion a woman had multiple
sclerosis and her left knee would not bend. She was healed in the name of Jesus and walked without pain any
longer. We walked all over together 'thanking Jesus'.

"Went back to work Saturday, November 23rd and
told the girls what Jesus did and they can't tease me any
more about pigeon-toes. I even had to get new shoes.
Thank God, I don't hurt anymore when I get off work.

"People are coming to me about healing and I am no
longer afraid to stand up for Jesus because He has given
us all power by the Holy Spirit to care for others and love
those who don't believe as I believe. I hurt when they
hurt and praise God when they're healed!"

An Exciting Church Becomes Really Excited

"First of all, I want to tell you what a blessing the
Denver Healing Explosion was to me. The Lord did some
special things for me just to be able to make it to the
teaching, and my healing partner and I had a BALL laying hands on the sick and getting them healed. We gig-

gled with joy the whole time.

"We saw arms and legs grow out for almost everyone and had one lady who had no sense of smell who had such a surprised look on her face as she smelled the perfume on Marcella's (my healing partner) arm.

"There were fifty to sixty people from our church who participated and everyone was still walking two feet off the ground when we got to church on Sunday morning. Our church is one of the most 'Full-of-the-Holy Spirit' churches in the world and I can see what an impact this *new teaching on healing* is going to have on the body of Christ in our area. *It is so exciting!* Thank you for being persistent and obedient to the Lord in your teaching."

"I Caught The Vision!"
John Webb, pastor of the International Gospel Fellowship in Aurora, Colorado called just as we were completing this book with a tremendously exciting praise report. He dismissed his congregation the Wednesday night before Christmas, took his equipment and *all the members of his church who had been on the Denver Healing Explosion team.* They went to a nursing home and ministered in praise and worship and then he turned the "Hunter Healing Teams" lose on those aged people.

He said it was incredible to watch as the teams were growing out arms and legs, adjusting necks supernaturally as they were taught, getting people out of wheelchairs and having them walk, and performing scores of other exciting miracles by the power of God in the name of Jesus!

This is the most exciting type of miracle to us because it is the end-time ministry in action where people are healing people. We believe we are in the foothills of the age when *all believers* will be doing these types of miracles daily wherever they go. Pastor John Webb saw the vision God had given us and is running with this vision to complete the work of Jesus. He was our coordinator for the Denver Healing Explosion and worked as efficiently and vigorously in putting the details of the meeting together as he is continuing to do by putting the details of the ministry of the body of Christ together.

It's Better To Give Than To Receive
FROM GOLDEN, COLORADO: "There was a lady totally deaf in her right ear who had a hearing aid in the left. She said, 'Just work on the left ear' because she 'had some hearing there'. I told her Jesus wanted both ears healed. I bound and cast out the spirit of deafness. After removing the hearing aid, I leaned over and whispered in her ear, 'Can you hear me?'

"She replied, 'No! I told you I was totally deaf in that ear!' Jesus has a sense of humor, isn't that great?

"I'm awaiting x-rays to send proof to you. I was totally disabled from lumbar disc disease in 1972, and an auto accident five years later resulted in my shin bone (tibia) being broken in five places. The bones were not set, my leg was one inch short, the pain constant. But with a brace, one inch lift on my shoe and a cane, I could walk short distances. Charles healed me at Victory Church on the ORU campus in Tulsa, Oklahoma, and then I received the baptism with the Holy Spirit and spoke in tongues when he ministered. I began to witness to anyone and everyone I saw..a 'Jesus blabber-mouth'! And I led several people to Christ.

"*Thanks to you, my miracle has now gone full circle... from being healed and saved, to healing others and leading them to Christ. That's really what it's all about, isn't it?"*

Healing Is So Natural To The Believer
"Thank you so much for teaching and ministering to us in Denver this past week. As members of one healing team, my wife and I ministered healing to seven people at the Healing Explosion.

(1) One ten-year-old boy had pain in his leg from an accident at play. He was instantly healed and his face said it all. He will tell everyone Jesus healed him.

(2) A man with muscle spasms in his legs (right then and since he was born) was healed and his left leg lengthened.

(3) A woman with lumps in her chest came and was healed. The lumps disappeared or reduced in size immediately. She then told us she had never been slain in the Spirit and would like to be...she was out longer than anyone I have seen...God must have done even more in that twenty minutes, she was so grateful and full of love toward Him when she got up.

(4) Two different women came with arthritis and were in pain; both were healed. While neither were advanced cases of the disease, both were convinced of their healing because of the pain leaving and the heat in their joints, legs and back.

(5) One woman had back pain from an automobile accident. We commanded her back to be healed as we checked her legs. Her right leg was short, it grew out and the pain left.

(6) Best for Last — A grandmother in the stadium seats who could not get to the floor had been baptized with the Holy Spirit earlier in the evening. She had pain in her left side, a ruptured stomach which she said was painful all of the time. The rupture was discernible as a

golf ball size lump below her sternum. She had emphysema, and a spirit of fear made her cower like a
mouse in her seat.

We bound the spirit of fear and commanded it to
leave and loved her for a minute or two. Then we commanded the pain in her side to go and commanded healing of that area. Her face lit up and she said it had gone.
She had quit smoking several months ago so we spoke a
new set of lungs into her. When we commanded her to
breathe deeply and receive her new lungs, I didn't think
she was going to stop inhaling. Her eyes lit up again. She
was so shocked that she had been healed that we stopped
for a second and let her just thank the Lord.

Her prayer language began to flow as she praised
Him. Then we commanded a new stomach lining and
supporting tissue to be created, the ruptured area to be
just like God had created it originally and rebuked pain
from her. She was healed of this also and when we
checked her arms, one was short and we commanded it to
grow out and it did. She was then instructed to tell of her
healings and not allow the devil to come and quench her
faith.

"November 24, Sunday after the Healing Explosion:
At church this morning one young man had bone grown
back into his jaw, the dentist told him he would lose a
tooth because of gum disease. He won't. His wife checked
his mouth and said the swelling was gone!

"One girl received the baptism of the Holy Spirit...and best of all we saw that a group of people who had
attended the 'Explosion' were not 'praying for the sick'.
They had seen enough to minister healing with authority. I'm sorry I don't have the results of their ministry but
we will encourage them. One woman among this group
said God had spoken to her during the time of ministry

and said, 'Barbara, don't ever go back to the other way of
healing the sick!'

"Your teaching ministry to me began in 1979 when I
went up to help as a catcher and ended up being able to
lean over Charles' shoulder while he ministered to about
seventy-five people. I saw enough that one night to go
back and begin ministering to the sick with authority.
That one night back in 1979 resulted in my being able to
minister to my own family, seeing arms and legs grow out
and devils cast out and a case of cancer (diagnosed as terminal) healed, arthritis cast out, and backs healed.
Thanks, Charles, for showing me."

Love and Appreciation,
Bob and Wanda

Work, For The Night Is Coming

"Harvest since the afternoon session!

(1) Prayed (commanded!) for my friend who was
very ill:

   a) Healed of crushing pressure on chest (was a *spirit*,
not her medication)!

   b) Word of knowledge my son gave: Unseen lump on
her throat healed and gone!

   c) Under the power in the Lord! (My first time someone has been blessed like that when praying for the
sick.) Praise the Lord!

(2) New boldness: Passed a serious accident on the
way to Wyatt's Cafeteria, turned around and went back
to pray for the man. Placed in ambulance just as we
reached him. We stood there as a family and prayed anyway. Thank You, Jesus!

(3) Began sharing with a stranger (loving woman) in
line at Wyatt's about the Holy Spirit. We ate dinner together and right in Wyatt's we prayed for her to receive

the baptism of the Holy Spirit and she showed the manifestation of tongues (with tears of joy). We now have a
beautiful sister in the Lord who is a Spirit-filled *Quaker!*
Praise the Lord! She's planning on coming tonight to listen and tomorrow also.

"Thank You, Jesus! Thank you, Charles and
Frances! God Bless You!"

Continued To Minister Every Day

"I was so thrilled with the Healing Explosion — not
only with what God did through simple everyday people,
but the impact it has made on my ministry and others in
the Denver area.

"There were thirty people from Abundant Word
who were trained and were on the healing teams on Friday night. Most of these people will continue to minister
in our weekly team ministry times and will be actively
training others. They are so excited about this mighty
new way of serving Jesus.

"My sister attended and after receiving ministry, fell
under the power. She had poor circulation in her legs and
both were swollen and painful. While lying on the floor,
she felt her feet shrinking in her shoes and when she got
up her shoes were too large and she even had trouble
walking in them. The team that had ministered were
busy with someone else, so she could not tell them what
happened, even though they had seen her leg grow out.

"I have continued to minister to people everyday
since the Healing Explosion with power evident each
time. Thank you for coming to Denver and allowing us to
take part. We are bold and excited and God's healing has
just begun!! We love you both."   Ruth

The "HUNTER" Healing Methods — Really Jesus

"Our first 'patient' was a young gal in her twenties who was suffering from neck pain, lower back pain, ulcers, and unforgiving heart due to rape. My first thought was 'Hallelujah!' (like Frances always says). We ministered the healing techniques we learned through our studies and seminar with you, and she was totally healed and slain in the Spirit. Praise Jesus! The most significant miracle was the healing of the damaged emotions and broken heart caused by rape and unforgiveness.

"Our next patient was a gentleman in his sixties who had epilepsy, shoulder and spinal arthritis, a hiatal hernia, and a concussion (from a recent fall). He was all stiffened up when he walked up to us, exhibiting obvious pain. We ministered our Hunter-taught healing techniques and, praise Jesus, the poor man was set free. In his joy and excitement he kept saying that he could feel the fluid coming into his joints as he waved his arms over his head for the first time in years. What a thrill to be in the service of Jesus!

"Another 'patient' of ours was a young gal with an eight-year-old son. She had cancer and the doctors gave her only six months to live. Also she was suffering from deafness, diverticulitis, varicose veins, and intense pain. We renounced that bad report of death and commanded the spirit to leave along with the spirit of cancer and the spirit of deafness. One of those spirits came out the top of her head and shot straight up through the top of the Coliseum. Wow, what a sight! Praise Jesus! We continued to minister to her the 'Hunter healing methods' and she was set free. Her hearing was restored, the pain was gone, and she felt sure that she was totally healed. She even gave her testimony on stage with Frances. Praise the Lord!"   Trig and Beve Jo

A Jesus Overhaul

"Praise the Lord and thank you for coming to Denver and having the Healing Explosion! I'm healed!

"I didn't look a mess but I was! Although I have many times laid hands on the sick and seen God healing through me, and been healed too, and even worked with a Messianic evangelist with a healing ministry, I was still sick! I felt so awful that I didn't know what to believe God for. I went to a nutritionist and chiropractor and was doing some better. But, I had so many symptoms and side effects I didn't even know what to ask for until one of the training meetings when God showed me why the confusion.

"*God gave me* a new pancreas (no more hypoglycemia!); a new liver; cleaned my blood of candida albicans (a fungus that's terrible and caused confusion, etc.); dissolved the clots in my blood which were keeping the blood from getting to organs and making me feel unmotivated and lacking in energy.

"HALLELUJAH! I feel great! I'm just thirty-nine years of age and I've never been a quitter, but I've felt so terrible for years. But no more! I must keep my diet right and stay out of stress...no problem with Jesus!

Now for the icing. I went back to the nutritionist to ask her to do another test on my blood because God healed me. She was sweet and did it — three times. Of course the proof is in the clear blood! Hallelujah!"   Linda

God's Blessings Flow

"I will mention three of the healings that took place through me by the power of the Holy Spirit during the Denver Healing Explosion.

"The first person I ministered to was a lady. She said she had stomach pains and I could see a nervousness in her face. I told her God has not given her a spirit of fear, but of love, and of power, and a sound mind. In Jesus' name, I commanded the spirit of fear to leave, and immediately the spirit left because I could see it in her eyes; she smiled, her countenance changed, and a joy and peace was evident on her face.

"She then told me she had leg pain, her knees hurt, and she had 'hammer toes' which I had never heard of. I sat her down and grew out her leg about one-half inch. But when she stood up she said her knees hurt and she still had her 'hammer' toes. I stood her back on the carpet and in Jesus' name commanded the back to be healed, the muscle, knees, and feet to be healed in Jesus' name.

"I laid hands on her forehead and she went out under the power; she sat up and touched her knees. She started to cry. Then she stood up and said something, but I could not understand her because of her crying and the noise. She then stood up and said to me, 'My feet are healed! I was in excruciating pain when I came down here, but now the pain is all gone!' She started to praise the Lord and I received a blessing. I told her to go to the platform and tell what happened. She just continued to praise the Lord and cry. A little later I told her again to go to the platform and you, Frances, told everyone to listen to her healing testimony. She was one of the first ones to come to the platform. It wasn't until just then when I realized what happened. Praise the Lord!

"My healing team partner's son came to us and told me he had scoliosis. In Jesus' name I commanded the spirit of scoliosis to come out and I put my fingers behind his neck at the base of the skull. I felt heat there and in Jesus' name commanded the spine to straighten and to be healed. He went out under the power of the Holy Spirit. When he came out from under the power of the Holy Spirit, he said, 'The pain is gone.' I knew he was healed. Praise the Lord!

"This experience, so far, is the highlight of my Christian walk. I will continue to heal the sick. Thank you, Jesus!"
                                                            David

We Were Teaching Others Already!

"Cheryl and I were back sharing with our church and fellow believers some of these things that happened. Immediately, a lady raised her hand for healing of a wrist and hand. We spoke the healing in Jesus' name and the numbness began to leave, the skin looked normal and strength began to return to the hand. Later, a man came forward for healing a bad headache. The visiting speaker asked if someone from the body of believers could be instructed by us to give the healing command! WE WERE TEACHING OTHERS ALREADY!

"So, a teenage girl came forward who has the baptism of the Holy Spirit and we told her what to say and the man's headache left! Then, this man wanted to do the NEXT HEALING!...a lady with a swollen finger and some kind of a cyst. Then, we told him what to say and how to grow out arms! It was exciting!!! The arm grew out, and the finger began to return to normal.

"Since Sunday, Cheryl and I each had a chance to minister healing to injured eyes and the manifestation came right away! One of these people was my young nephew who really does not know Jesus. We gave Jesus all the glory and my little nephew just could not believe that Jesus would heal him, but He did! Praise the Lord!

"As you can see, this is a wonderful beginning! Cheryl and I are believing for an EXPLOSION of miracles of healing and salvation and baptism of the Holy Spirit in our city. Thank you, thank you, thank you for

teaching us, the everyday believer, how to heal the sick!
"HALLELUJAH! We love you!"   Joy and Cheryl

Don't Pass Up An Opportunity
"We wanted to be faithful to our commitment to write you of the wonderful works of our Lord at the Denver Healing Explosion.

"My husband and I ministered to a lady with burning on her legs and curled toes. We grew out her legs and arms and the toes straightened. She was amazed and praised the Lord.

"A young man in his twenties wanted healing for a severely damaged optic nerve in his left eye. He was legally blind in that eye. We ministered healing to his legs first and he then told us he had been run over by a car at age two and his spine was out of line, even his face was not straight in line with his body. As we ministered to his arms and neck, his spine straightened and he began to say, 'I see blue color and people moving about.' We laid hands on him again and commanded the optic nerve to be healed. He still had blurred vision but we rejoiced and thanked Jesus together.

"We prayed and anointed the pictures of two children for one lady and claimed financial increase for her, a single parent.

"A ten-year-old boy wanted his leg healed where his mother had closed the door on it. He was in pain and limping. We grew out his legs and commanded the pain to go, and he was healed — free of pain and no limp. Praise the Lord!

"I was really touched by your ministering the love of Jesus and sharing the things you all have learned. It just makes me want to go and do.

"Today, I did invite my neighbor to go with me to an

Aglow meeting. She could not, but said she had been by to see me and I was not home. Then she asked what I had been doing. I told her learning to heal the sick and shared how we learned from you. Then she said, 'My back has been killing me.' What an opportunity!

"To make a long story short, after my meeting was over I dropped by her house, ministered healing to her legs, arms and neck with much heat from my hands and she was healed and amazed. Then I shared Jesus with her, led her in salvation and the baptism of the Holy Spirit with the evidence of speaking in tongues. Praise God. Her comment was, 'I hope I feel this way forever.'"

Darrell and Jean

The Most Exciting Day Of My Life
"The Denver Healing Explosion was the most exciting day of my life! I may never get married now, that experience would pale next to the Explosion!

"A lady told me she had trouble with her back and wanted to be delivered from the spirit of nicotine. I said, 'No problem!' I grew out her arms (to my amazement), then grew her legs out (the adrenaline is now pumping like mad!!!) I told her, 'Stand up. How do you feel?'

"She said, 'WONDERFUL, THE PAIN IS GONE!!' By now my heart is beating so wildly with excitement I think I've grown a bra size!!!!(only temporarily).

"I practically yelled, 'FANTASTIC!!! Now let's get rid of that spirit!!'

"She said to me, 'All right! Let's GO!!' and jumped onto the carpet. I bound that thing in the name of Jesus (meanwhile my partner was talking to her and telling her to praise the Lord and say, thank you, Jesus!!) Well, she concentrated on what I was saying to her, Praise the Lord, and fell under the power when I cast that spirit out by the power of the Holy Spirit.

"A man came up to me and told me, 'Oh, I have plenty of problems. I don't know where to start.' I didn't know this man had scoliosis. He said, 'I have a mis-aligned spine, pain in my neck, shoulders and lower back and I would like to be delivered from the spirit of lust.'

"I told him, 'THAT'S EASY, NO PROBLEM!'" I grew his arms out and used Charles' method on his neck. I sat him down and was shocked to find out his left leg was almost a full inch shorter than the right, if not just a tad more. He was surprised too!! Well, I commanded that leg to GROW!!! As we both started cheering (I'm an ex-cheerleader and haven't forgotten my training!), his leg got a little carried away. I guess it got excited too!!! But we caught it before it went too far. Before I could completely say, 'GET BACK THERE!!', it had snapped back into place. This little guy was laughing hysterically.

"I said, 'Jump up and tell me how you feel.'

"He told me, 'ABSOLUTELY FANTASTIC!!!' I could have done a spiritual BOOGIE all the way back to Connecticut (but I decided to take the plane)! I got him back on the rug and caught the attention of the usher.

"With one hand on his shoulder and the other on his head I bound and cast out the spirit of lust and he fell under the power. When he got up he didn't want to leave!!! He showed me a wart on his knee; I sent that away. He pulled up the other pants leg and showed me scar tissue; and we got rid of that ! He finally stood up and said, 'Well, I do have this cut on my finger I got this morning. It still hurts,' and he laughed again. I couldn't help being amused, but Jesus loves that finger as the rest of the body. We didn't want that finger to get jealous. It healed.

"Yours Lovingly in Christ,"   Verdell

The New Realm Of The Supernatural

"God is so good! I am so thankful for your obedience to the call the Lord has on your lives.

"Truly the Healing Explosion was the doorway into a new realm of the supernatural. The night of the Explosion was electrical with expectation from the people in the Coliseum!

"My partner and I ministered healing to six people. The most spectacular was a teenage girl who had Reyes Syndrome. She was there with her mother and her best friend. Her mother was being ministered to on our left, and her friend to the right. They had come from Erie, Colorado with great expectation!

"The girl didn't know anything about this disease. She was only concerned with the fact that it had caused scar tissue on her scalp. She was unable to grow hair in the area. You know how much appearance means to a teenager.

"So after a few preliminaries, we got down to business (with the devil). I bound that spirit. I commanded restoration to her brain cells, nerves, etc. Then I spoke directly to the scar tissue and commanded it to dissolve, and for hair to be restored. I then thanked the Lord, touched her on her forehead, and she went out.

"She got up weak and shaking at the knees. She wept and hugged me. We sat her down where she proceeded to remove her coat because she was so hot! The power of God was *all over* her! I know she got healed. I know it!

"I carefully listened to your exhortation telling us to make this laying on of hands a lifestyle; to look for opportunities everywhere. I also received from the Spirit the prophecy at the breakfast. He said because of my commitment He would send fire to burn out anything that's not of Him. One thing I had that was not of Him was a fear of man, a fear of what they think. But like Charles said, 'When they see a miracle, they'll believe.'

"So I made a decision that I was going to move out in boldness. I'm always around sick people. I work in a V.D. clinic. Monday morning a co-worker started her usual complaints of bursitis. I told her what I learned about that. I laid hands on her. God healed her. She wept. Now I'm believing she'll get on fire for Jesus.

"Another co-worker is deaf. I laid hands on him. No manifestation yet, but he gave his life to the Lord! He asked Jesus to come in!! Glory!"   Audrey

Keep Your Spirit Open To God

"As a healing team member at the Denver Healing Explosion, several highlights made the experience unforgettable and life-transforming. The opportunity to step out in faith and operate in the Spirit was exciting.

"The presence of the Holy Spirit all evening was so powerful and so beautiful tears came to my eyes several times. It was such a faith builder to see God move so magnificently and to see myself as a servant of His. I thank the Lord again and again for your obedience to His vision of seeing believers everywhere move out and minister healing to the world.

"My healing partner and I ministered to a number of people, mainly for back pain and also through prayer cloths for family members who were sick or needed to know Jesus. The highlight for me was ministering to a young woman whose hips and shoulders were uneven in opposite directions. After we grew out her arms and legs and saw some improvement, she said she wanted to check her hips and then would return if they didn't appear more even. She did come back and after talking

with her some more, my partner ministered a creative
miracle for a broken collar bone she received as a child,
evening her shoulders some more.

"After we ran out of ways to minister to her, my
partner said she wished the girl would go out under the
power. As I stood behind the girl I felt impressed to ask
her if she had forgiveness in all her relationships. (This is
the first time we received and acted on a word of knowledge.) When I asked her, she said by faith she forgave a
certain person during the prayer led earlier in the evening for everyone to pray. We stood in agreement with her
that she had forgiven this person and before we finished,
she went out under the power! "   Johnne

The Spirits Quake

"The Healing Explosion in Denver will never be forgotten in my heart and mind. It is one of the most significant events in my Christian experience. The training
and the actual healing by us has added tremendous confidence to me. Then the baptism with fire during the Victory Breakfast has killed 'self', so obeying God to do the
works that He wants me to do is so possible and believ-
able now. Praise God! The significant miracles during
the Healing Explosions are the following:

"A teenager came to my partner and me with redness
in her right eye. She said the doctor said that it was arthritis or a syphilitic symptom. I cast out the spirit of arthritis and cursed the seed of syphilis and caused it to
die, then ministered healing to the eye. I also cast out the
spirit of fear and invited the Lord's peace and love to
flood her and cleanse her. She was a new person when
she left, praise God!

"A three-year-old girl was brought to us. The
mother said that the girl's adenoids were so swollen that

the doctor said he would have to operate. She was having difficulty breathing. I touched the nose area and said, 'Be healed in the name of Jesus', and the adenoids decreased in size and she could breathe much easier. Thank You, Jesus! Her mother had a tipped uterus. My partner grew out her legs and at the same time her uterus was put into the right position. Praise the Lord!

"A man and lady came up to us with objects to be anointed for a son who had left home and was on drugs and another son with dyslexia, low self concept and social skills. We prayed believing and know that each situation will be resolved!

"One of the marshals had back problems and arthritis in his knees. My partner grew out his legs, arms and adjusted his neck and spine and cast out the spirit of arthritis. He was fine — Thank You, Jesus!

"It was a wonderful experience and just a beginning for further ministry.

"Thank you so much for obeying God and following His Holy Spirit. *The evil spirits are quaking with the newly revived power in us.*"

Bless you,
Karen

Blind Eyes Opened

FROM BOULDER, COLORADO: "I was on a healing team in the 'Holy Ghost' Healing Explosion in Denver. I've been thinking over all that happened on Friday and I have seen so much growth in my own faith and boldness because of what the Holy Spirit did through my hands and the hands of other 'ordinary' believers.

"My team partner and I met the afternoon before the meeting for the first time. She is from Dallas, Texas. We encouraged each other and words of knowledge would come from each of us for the people's healing.

"When the first lady came up I was a bit nervous. She had allergies and showed me her arms, where there were scratch marks and discoloration under her fingernails. She said she also itched internally and was pregnant, too! I said, 'That's easy!' I followed what we had been taught and laid hands on her and asked her where the itching had gone.

"Her eyes lit up and she smiled brightly and said, 'It's gone!' After that, it was easy. My faith was strengthened and I knew that anything was possible to him who believes on the name of Jesus! Hallelujah!

"My partner was ministering to a lady who had back problems and the lady's husband was standing next to me waiting for his wife, I thought. I told him that it would all be taken care of that night, and tears came to his eyes as he said, 'That's what I've been waiting for.' I thought he was talking about his wife, but, praise God, he had a cataract behind his left eye and had lost most of his sight in the eye. He was going to have it operated on on December 5th. I laid hands on this precious man and in Jesus' name commanded the cataract to dissolve, and progressively he said, 'It's going away.' Finally, it *totally dissolved* and he said, 'I can see!' We jumped all over praising God! Praise Jesus!"   Sandy

Steel Doesn't Bend — Or Does It?
"Praise the Lord!!! We were blessed by the teaching and ministry at the Denver Healing Explosion this last weekend.

"The first person we ministered to was a young woman who told us she was hypoglycemic and that her pancreas and adrenal glands were not functioning properly. I was not sure what the adrenal gland was so I commanded a new pancreas and adrenal gland to replace the old. She said she truly felt she had received a new pancreas and went up on the platform and stated she no longer felt 'jittery'.

"A couple then stopped in front of us who wanted prayer for their children who were having marital problems and their grandchild who was ill at home. After speaking healing to the marriage and health to the child, the woman wanted ministry for herself and her husband. It was like they were testing the 'water'. First a toe and then a foot, then finally jumping in completely! Hallelujah!

"The husband said he had a defective valve in his heart. After commanding a new valve to come in we asked if he had anything else wrong in his body. He said he had lower back pain. Come to find out he had two steel rods in his back. We first checked his arms and legs and found them to be even. A voice (you know whose) came to me and said, 'You're not going to help him.' I thought, 'Oh, yes we are!' We had heard the testimony of Norma Jean LeRoy who had been healed with rods in her back and able to touch her toes. After we spoke healing to his back he said the pain was gone and he bent down and touched his toes. Thank You, Jesus! He said he was unable to do that before Friday night. Dr. Owellen verified his healing and he said his back had been injured in an automobile accident five years ago.

"We have continued to see the Lord work through our hands the last two days since the 'Explosion' and give Him all the praise and glory."

Glen and Barbara

Never Give Up
"A grateful thank you for all the wonderful hours of training and inspiration at the recent Denver Healing

Explosion. Thank you for sharing what the Lord has taught you and for sharing His vision for this work of healing the nations. The music and praise were also such a blessing, and the praise and worship before the Friday night meeting began were especially powerful in preparing for the ministry during the meeting.

"My healing partner and I ministered to a young man who had recurring warts and eczema. We cursed the seed of both, bound and commanded the release of both from his body permanently, and they did as commanded. I then placed one hand on his abdomen and the other on the small of his back, and a powerful surge of heat passed into him as the Holy Spirit filled him with love. My partner spoke to him that he was clean in the sight of the Lord, and not dirty. He went under the power, and when he got up, he couldn't get over the love he was feeling. He hugged us both several times with such a radiant smile on his face. Hallelujah.

"We delivered a teenage girl from inherited spirits of back pain and sway-back and commanded the spine and all vertebrae, muscles, tendons, nerves and tissues to adjust. Praise God, all pain left her body and her back straightened. She had experienced pain for as long as she could remember as a small child. Her parents were with her and concurred that she had pain from early childhood.

"My partner has been in severe pain since she injured her back before Easter last spring. She was ministered to at the Explosion but continued to have severe pain. I ministered to her yesterday morning, and all pain left her body as all the vertebrae, muscles, etc. adjusted, and her hips and pelvis rotated into place. Glory to God!

"Thank you again for being God's yielded and enthusiastic servants equipping the saints for ministering healing." Trinah

Vision Restored

"Decided to write you a letter and let you know what happened on our team during the Healing Explosion, as promised.

"Our first 'patient' complained of head pain related to a sinus condition. Steve held her head as Charles had taught and commanded the sinuses to be healed. She was healed immediately.

"We waited several minutes before the next person came. He was wearing glasses and indicated that his vision had grown steadily worse during the past several months. I asked him if he had any other problems — specifically if he had any back problems. He said he had hurt his back several months ago but it didn't bother him very much. I grew his arms out and laid hands on his eyes commanding them to be healed — no results. I then had him sit down and grew his leg out about an inch. He indicated the back pain was gone but his eyes were no better. I asked Steve what he thought we should do next. He held the man's head and neck as Charles taught and the vision was restored. Praise God!

"I would like to thank you very much for bringing the Healing Explosion to Denver and teaching us. We will share God's healing power with others even as you shared with us." Sam

My First Time To Minister Healing

"Greetings in Jesus' name. I am so overwhelmed by the visible glory of God shown in the Healing Explosion until I can't cease from talking and praising the Lord for His miraculous blessings, and to think that God used *ordinary me* to be a part of His healing team is just awesome.

"I just thank and glorify Him for His great and wonderful love. My life will never be the same again. Praise the Lord!

"Let me attempt to tell you briefly about my experiences. My partner and I laid hands and ministered healing to four people who were healed.

"The first was a man in his forties. He had scoliosis — he complained that he had pain in his shoulders, head, neck, his hands were numb, etc. My partner commanded his vertebrae to line up and ordered the spirit of pain and scoliosis to come out. At first he said he was still in pain, so we continued to minister healing by commanding the spirit of scoliosis and pain to come out. The pain left his head and neck, but he complained the pain was still in his shoulder. We checked the length of his arms and then we told him to sit to check his leg lengths. The left leg was nearly an inch shorter than the right. I placed my hand on his feet and commanded the ligaments, bones, muscles, tissues, veins, and arteries to grow out in the name of Jesus. As soon as I said, 'In the name of Jesus', the leg leaped out in seconds. We began to thank and praise God. When he stood up again, the pains were all gone.

"He took off his glasses and began to cry, saying, 'I know God did something to me because I'm so closed, I've never been able to talk to anyone the way I talk to you. Because of my shyness, people shun me.' He then told us his hands were numb with no feeling. We rebuked the numbness and commanded it to come out, then feeling came into his hands except for the tip end of his fingers. We told him to praise God and the numbness would completely go away. He was just rejoicing and left praising God.

"The second experience involved a lady who had

sinus problems, nose drainage, pain in her head, and a lump in her throat. She had had this lump for a year. She had been to the doctor, but he couldn't discover the cause of the lump in her throat; also her four children at home were sick with the flu.

"My partner laid hands on her and commanded the spirit of pain and sinus problems to come out for a complete healing. The pain left her sinus region but she said the area under her right ear was sore and painful, so I laid my hand on the spot that was sore and in pain as I laid my hands on both sides of her cheeks. I could feel the right jaw bone was higher and protruded more than the left. I questioned her about my observation. She said she had an overbite. I commanded the jawbone and teeth to line up in the name of Jesus, and it did. She told us she heard the bone snap back into place. The soreness also left from under her ear.

"We asked her about the lump in her throat. She said it was still there, but it was getting smaller. She could tell from swallowing. We gave a last command for the complete dissolving of that lump and told her to start praising and thanking God that she was healed.

"Our third experience was when a young man in his late teens came up to us and said, 'I want you to pray for healing of my heart. I have had pain in my heart for six months.' He had sprained his lumbar vertebrae on his job and his back had been painful for one year. He said he had been seeing a chiropractor, but to no avail. I commanded the spirit of pain to come out of him in Jesus' name and commanded complete healing of his heart and lumbar vertebrae, also for his spinal column to line up as God intended it to be. I then laid hands over his heart and asked him if he felt any pain.

"He replied, 'No, it's all gone.'

"I said, 'How do you feel?'

"He said, 'I feel good,' with amazement in his face and excitement in his voice.

"I then said, 'Let's praise the Lord for healing your heart and back! Now we will minister healing for deliverance from cigarettes.'

"I proceeded to command the spirit of lust and addiction to come out of him and never return in his body. Also said that he will not have any further desire for cigarettes. As I said, 'In the name of Jesus', my fingertips slightly touched his forehead. To my surprise, he just went back under the power of the Holy Ghost. I had to hastily help my partner catch him to prevent him from falling on another person who had fallen under the power and laid too close to us.

"After some minutes, he got up praising God and thanked us. We asked him if he was born again. He said, 'Yes.' We told him to go on his way praising God.

"I am on fire for the Lord, this zeal cannot be quenched. I am asking God for guidance to lead me where He wants me to witness for Him and spread this good news of the kingdom.

"I have had healing experiences on my person, but this is the first time I have ministered healing to another."   Miriam

"P.S. Do you know that I bought your book 'To Heal the Sick' when you were here at Happy Church, I believe, in September. I didn't want to lay it down until I had completed it. About two a.m. I woke up and started reading. The more I would read, the more my faith increased. The evening before, I had spilled some black dye on the oatmeal colored rug in our bedroom. It looked horrible on the rug. I put some clorox on a piece of cloth and rubbed the soiled rug to get the color out...the black color came out, but that particular area was bleached and turned white. I was even more upset because we are renting and had to put a sizeable deposit down. I showed my husband what had happened. He said, "Don't worry, tomorrow I'll try to get some information how I can get that bleached area dyed.

"While reading your book that morning, the Bible verse, Mark 11:23, became so alive, I jumped out of bed, went over to the vanity in our room where the rug was bleached white, commanded the color to be restored in the name of Jesus and the color began to change in front of my eyes. I knelt down and touched the rug and the beige color kept coming into the rug until it was completely restored. I started praising the Lord, woke my husband up and showed him what God had done. I explained that Jesus said you can have anything you ask if you don't doubt. This was about four a.m. We are still talking about the miracle."

He Slept Beautifully

"First of all, I want to thank you both for your encouragement. Without you, I may not have tried it.

"My brother-in-law who had four cancellations of his plane coming out from Seattle was miraculously given a ticket by an agent who overrode the computer to get him on a plane...the first miracle. The second was when the healing team lady laid hands on him, heat went through his heart and liver and he was slain powerfully in the Spirit. This is a thirty-five-year-old father who has three small sons. A year ago they told him he would have to have a heart transplant.

"He slept beautifully that night and praise God, the next day and ever since. The terrible difficulty in his breathing was gone. We believe he was totally healed! The next morning he was 'born again' at Wally and Mari-

lyn's Happy Church.
       "Praise God! We love you!"   Delores and Family

Greater Works Than These

"I want to thank you both for your faithfulness and willingness to serve the Lord Jesus Christ. It was several years ago in Greeley, Colorado that Charles laid hands on me to receive the baptism of the Holy Spirit. My life has never been the same.

"Now you have been led by God's Holy Spirit to bring to the body of Christ a school of healing with 'hands on' experience. Many in the body have been a-fraid to minister to the sick, and among those who have dared, many of us have been confused in how to accomplish this much-needed ministry. I praise God that through you He has chased the confusion away and has created an army to go forth boldly, armor in place, to take back what Satan has stolen and proclaim the Good News of Jesus.

"The first person my wife and I ministered to was a young man with back problems. He had had a disc removed and it caused pain off and on. Also, his wrist had been broken and had not healed properly. My wife, Nita, ministered to his short arm and it grew out. As I commanded his back to line up and be healed, his legs grew out even. We believe that God healed his back and wrist.

"A woman then who had had a mastectomy wanted to have her breast restored. Nita ministered to her, and the next morning the woman said she felt heat and pressure — the breast was beginning to reconstruct!

"Our oldest son Daniel (nine years old) was there to receive healing for congenitally dislocated hips. He was running around the Coliseum faster and faster praising God with tears of happiness. There is more manifestation of that healing taking place and *he is already at least an inch taller than he was.*

"A friend who came 150 miles to Denver wanted healing for the paralysis she has due to a stroke seven years ago. She is able to lift her left arm and her left foot faces forward for the first time since the stroke. Today she went to the doctor because she was suddenly so short of breath that fear began to creep in — we ministered peace to her before she went. The doctor could find nothing amiss and decided she is allergic to her heart medication — praise God! The women who ministered to her on Friday spoke a new heart into existence!

"In closing, I will relay a comment my father made on Sunday morning. He was not on the team but had come and brought others to the Friday night Healing Explosion.

"'There may possibly have been some more healed if Charles and Frances and a dozen other regionally or nationally known men and women of faith were the ones ministering but the effects of hundreds of people going forth to lay hands on the sick will soon make the number of healings in Denver on the twenty-second of November seem small.'

"God bless you!"   Richard and Nita

by Charles and Frances

As Charles looked at the eager trained teams alert for the signal to start their healing ministry in the Denver Healing Explosion, God impressed him that just as Jesus said, "The works that I do he (the believer) will do also; and greater works than these he will do", God was saying to us, "Greater works will the healing teams do than the works I have done through Charles and Frances!"

We get tremendously excited when we realize that those heavenly words of Jesus are coming true as the great multitudes of believers are finally learning how to perform miracles for Jesus, and are doing them! We were delighted with the note from Richard and Nita about their father's comment in the letter above.

Chapter Fourteen

The Great Physician
Works Through Physicians

For years in the ministry where God has mightily moved in healing the sick, we have always taken advantage of every opportunity to talk with medical doctors, chiropractors, and nurses as well as anyone else in the medical field. We know that they have much vital information, knowledge and wisdom about the human body and mind, and we have gleaned every bit of information we could from them. Jesus had a physician, Luke, on his team when He held *HEALING EXPLOSIONS* on earth, teaching His disciples *how to heal the sick!*

It is very important to say that in no way are we attempting to become equipped as doctors or nurses, but we have learned that the more you know about the causes and effects of sicknesses and diseases which come against a human, the more you can accomplish in divine healing. Just as a doctor must diagnose the cause and presence of a disease or affliction in his patients, it helps us also to know at least something about what is wrong with a person who comes to us for healing.

Jesus mentioned praying amiss. We have progressed in great strides by learning how to dispense and apply the healing power of God directly into the problem area. In the case of terminal illness, incurable because of not knowing the cause or cure, we found that we must cast out the evil spirit which causes it. If a demon spirit is the cause, and you attempt to heal without casting it out, you will be ministering amiss.

If a bone is broken and you cast a spirit out, it won't work. You must command the bone to come back together in Jesus' name and lay hands on the bone to allow the healing power of God's Holy Spirit to do the mending.

Jesus cast out spirits such as deafness, dumbness, blindness, epilepsy and insanity, and the sick were healed. We must follow His example and in order to do so, we must learn to identify or discern the presence of an evil spirit and what it has caused or brought on a person.

Jesus healed all manner of diseases and afflictions. He did this in many ways and combination of ways. We see Him speak to sicknesses, lay hands on the sick, have the sick put their faith into action in addition to many other ways of ministering healing.

Jesus clearly said that it was not by His power that He accomplished healings and deliverance, but it was by the power of His Father. He also said we would receive this same power when the Holy Spirit came upon us, and that we would then do the same miracles He did, and even greater ones because He was going to the Father and sending back the Holy Spirit to endue us with this heaven-sent power.

We have been blessed and thrilled by having many medical doctors, chiropractors, dentists, nurses and others in the medical field work with us in these wonderful Healing Explosions. The doctors' panels have been mighty in teaching both the doctors and us believers. We have learned considerably more than we ever knew about healing because of what God revealed through them, and the doctors and nurses have learned much about the divine application of healing.

We want you to have the pleasure and blessing of reading some of their reports. Enjoy them, and then move forward in ministering healing in a new adventure with Jesus!

Dr. Richard Owellen
Richard Owellen, Ph.D. in organic chemistry,
M.D., was associate professor of oncology at
Johns Hopkins Oncology Center, Johns Hop-
kins Medical School.

We were blessed to have Dr. and Mrs. Owellen on our doctors' panel which was one of the highlights of the Pittsburgh meeting. He was the physician who went to a Kathryn Kuhlman service as a skeptic and saw his own daughter healed, and then appeared in one of her books. Both Dr. Owellen and Rose worked with Kathryn for many years after that.

Their comments are well worth reading.

Dear Charles and Frances,

We could never begin to tell you what a thrill it was working with you in the Healing Explosion. That was a service unparalleled in Christian history, and we felt privileged to be a part of it. Needless to say, we are looking forward to the next one with anticipation, as it will undoubtedly be even greater than the first.

The two days of meetings in Pittsburgh beforehand were a particular blessing, and, we felt, added much valuable knowledge and confidence to the healing teams over and above what had been learned from the teaching tapes and book. Certainly this training added a great deal to the success of the service. In fact, it was a real eye-opener to us when we began to realize how many different ways there are to heal the sick.

1. One of the most outstanding miracles we saw was the great number who received the baptism with the Holy Spirit. We had never seen great moves in this area because salvation and healing had previously been stressed more than the baptism. Salvation, the baptism with the Holy Spirit and healings were all high-lighted in the Healing Explosion.

We received a personal blessing from this because a brother-in-law and his whole family (six children) received and spoke in tongues. Another young lady had always felt somewhat embarrassed when speaking in tongues, but she said the Spirit was so powerful at the Healing Explosion that it was very natural for her to freely speak out loud in tongues.

2. Another outstanding thing we saw was that when all the healing teams started ministering and the thousands began streaming from the seats to them, it looked like organized chaos! But, there were so many, many miracles of healing and deliverance taking place through the hands of so many teams, mostly ordinary lay people, that it was incredible to watch. It seemed that it was over so quickly because of the exciting results of healing that suddenly there were no people left for ministry. We felt the teams would have loved to minister to another 20,000 people if all of Pittsburgh had come to the meeting.

3. There was supernatural build-up of faith and expectation in the healing team members as we worked and worshipped in the training meetings in the William Penn Hotel and Channel 40 TV. By the time the Healing Explosion started, the whole group was so triggered inside that they were ready to be turned loose against the devil's work. We felt that the teams didn't expect anyone to leave without being healed, and it seemed it happened almost that way. We have never seen so many healed by so many ordinary people, and with such a small amount of training on how to heal the sick. This must be God's timing to move the whole body of Christ into performing the Great Commission where they live and work. Glory to God!

4. An autistic child was brought to a team by its mother who asked if a doctor could help in ministry, one who understood the characteristics and needs of the child. I was called.

An autistic child will always be withdrawn from anyone who approaches them. Knowing this, I got down on my knees before the eight (or nine) year old and began to befriend him. The child began watching me and then reached out his little hand to touch me — a dramatic sign to a doctor.

I cast out the autistic spirit and commanded the brain to be restored in Jesus' name. The child looked directly in my eyes and then climbed upon my knee. His mother said, "That has to be God because he never would do that before."

Once the spirit is broken, the child must develop its own mind like any other little child. Psychiatrists often work five to ten years to accomplish what God had done in a few minutes! Hallelujhah!

HIS POWER THROUGH YOU

Rose:

A woman came to be healed of a spot (scar) on her eye which had been there for years and many doctors had examined her but could do nothing. God had given us a word about how the gifts of the Spirit would be in operation on the healing teams.

I considered ways to minister healing, but God indicated to grow out her arms. I took the woman's purse and put it on my own right shoulder while I ministered. Nothing happened to the eye. I said, "God, what'll I do now?" To the woman, I said, "Tell me about your family."

As she did, nothing came to me. Then the purse seemed to be so heavy it could have had an anvil in it. I said, "What's in your purse?"

She said, "Nothing special or heavy."

I replied, "There must be. Look in your purse and take out the first thing you see."

A picture of her grandson was right on top. Suddenly, hate and anger rose up in the woman's face and she said, "That child's mother is a Mormon. She won't go to church." etc. etc.

I quickly discerned the unforgiveness and ministered to her in a special prayer which included the words that she would release the unforgiveness and put it under the blood of Jesus because in her own heart she could not forgive. When the prayer was finished the woman opened her eyes and THE SPOT WAS GONE! Hallelujah!

By Charles and Frances

"Your heavenly Father will forgive you if you forgive those who sin against you; but if you refuse to forgive them, he will not forgive you" (Matthew 6:14,15

TLB).

"See, you have been made well. Sin no more, lest a worse thing come upon you" (John 5:14 NKJV).

Can just anyone who believes operate in the supernatural? Jesus simply said "Those who believe shall..." and the miracle reports are coming to us in vast numbers of the mighty miracles of the Healing Explosions! Glory to God!

Dr. Owellen and Rose have been a tremendous help in teaching at the Healing Explosions, as well as supervising teams and helping them when they did not get healing results. They have worked with us in all of the Healing Explosions to date. This is their Denver report:

It was fantastic!! I think Denver was the best Healing Explosion yet! The healing teams were very well organized and also well placed on the arena floor, and things went quite well.

Here are some of the healings that took place as can be recalled while things are still fresh in mind.

One of the healing team members ministered to a woman who had weakness and numbness in her one leg. She tried growing out the legs and commanding healing in Jesus' name, but there was no relief. She came to one of the supervisors for help. On further questioning it was discovered that the woman had had surgery on her leg when she was just a baby to remove several cysts. That surgery resulted in some of the nerves and muscles being severed. The woman felt that the doctor probably had made a mistake. It was pointed out that he probably *had* to do that kind of extensive surgery in order to remove the cyst. The healing team member then commanded new nerves and muscles to grow in the name of Jesus, and a restoration to take place, and immediately feeling and strength began to return to the leg.

This case seems to point out the importance of getting all the available information from the person needing healing, especially when healing does not occur with the first attempt. The next case repeats this same principle.

Another woman came to ask the question, "How do you minister to someone with a non-functioning thyroid gland?" It was explained that it is the same as a person with diabetes, where one speaks a new pancreas into the body in Jesus' name, only here one speaks a new thyroid. She then said that this was her problem, and she wanted to be healed. Healing was ministered, but there was no response. It was noted that the woman was very tense, and she appeared nervous and almost afraid.

More questions were then asked about the condition, and it was learned that the woman had had an overactive thyroid about fifteen years prior, and the doctor had given her radioactive iodine to slow down the thyroid. She then revealed that she was afraid that *she* had actually burned out her own thyroid, because she had been so active as a dancing teacher. It was explained that radioactive iodine frequently causes the thyroid to stop functioning after about fifteen to twenty years, and her activity had nothing to do with the thyroid stopping its function.

When she realized it was *not* because of her activity that the thyroid stopped, there was a tremendous flood of relief that came over her face and her whole countenance and attitude changed. She had felt guilty about this for the last two years and now the guilt was gone. When healing was ministered to her now in Jesus' name, she immediately fell under the power of God. As she lay there, she began to sob saying that she could feel a heat going through her neck. When she was seen the next day, she looked like a completely different person, alive and confident and active. Of course, she was told to continue her medicine until her doctor had checked her out, and *he* told her to come off the medication.

A healing team member came for help, since she and her partner had ministered healing repeatedly to a man with pain and "grinding" in his elbow and shoulder with no results. They had grown out his arms, bound and cast out the spirit of arthritis and commanded the body to be healed, but the pain and grinding remained. What they described sounded like bone grinding on bone, which would mean that there had been destruction of the joint structures. They were advised to command a new joint in the name of Jesus. Five minutes later they returned to report that the pain was gone, and so was the grinding, and the arm was completely free.

A woman came forward to testify, holding two hearing aids in her hand. She had been severely hard of hearing in both ears since birth, and to hear anything at all, she had to wear a hearing aid in each side. Someone on the healing teams ministered to her, and both ears were opened instantly. She could hear normal speech, even above the noise of the crowd, and she could hear a coarse whisper spoken behind her and understand what had been said.

A woman with bad arthritis throughout her body came for healing, and several of the young children from Nebraska (the ones who parade the banners) ministered to her. They cast out the spirit of arthritis in Jesus' name, and the pain and stiffness left her body. What a sight, to see the children and this elderly woman all crying and rejoicing together over what God had done for her.

There was a fifteen-year-old girl who had scoliosis,

and when healing was ministered to her by growing out her arms and legs, the pain left and her back appeared to be perfectly straight.

One very interesting situation occurred when a woman came up and stated that she had had her right lung surgically removed. When healing was ministered to her by commanding a new lung in Jesus' name, she could feel the air moving down into the right side of her chest and her breathing improved. Of course, this will need to be confirmed by her doctor. If it proves out, it will indeed be a most remarkable miracle.

Well, needless to say, we're already looking forward to Jacksonville, and our only regret is that we will have to wait 'til February for the next Healing Explosion.

The Lord bless you,   Rich and Rose Owellen

Dr. Roy J. LeRoy, Chiropractor

After forty years of treating the sick as a chiropractor, I see the work of the Lord as never before. It took me all these years to find out that the Lord could do the adjusting in the name of Jesus without my help! It saves a lot of work to let the Lord do the adjustment without my doing it manually.

Some of the miraculous things I saw...a dumb boy speaking for the first time in twenty years, a lady given up by the Mayo Clinic miraculously healed (the healing was verified by the doctors at the Mayo Clinic), a man of sixty with Parkinson's disease bent over and shuffling along with both hands shaking, suddenly straightened up, HEALED, and he took off running and dancing.

The things that happen at the Healing Explosions just boggle my mind. The healing teams come into the meeting expecting God to do what He says He'll do. When two or more are gathered together in His name, the

Father will do anything asked of Him, the Bible says. The healing teams are learning that they can minister healing to their neighbors, friends and to each other as long as they are in unity and agreement. I want to say that the reason the healing teams are so successful is because they are all in agreement and there are no scoffers present.

The main thing in being able to heal the sick is to apply the principles that the Hunters teach in the seminars and their book, "To Heal the Sick". These principles are taken from the scriptures and they work!!!

Norma Jean and I are grateful to be a part of this current mighty move of God.

In divine health,   Dr. Roy J. LeRoy

Norma Jean LeRoy

It was a joy to be at the first three Healing Explosions and to have a part in them. We attended the mini-explosion in Iowa also. We praise the Lord for the chance to be at each of these.

I saw more miracles this year between these Healing Explosions and your meetings in Minnesota than I have seen in all my previous life. At Pittsburgh all that God was doing was so wild that I could hardly comprehend it. I just walked around being a supervisor and saw numerous miracles and the place was just wild with praising the Lord and shouts of victory.

In my opinion, the Denver Explosion was the most exciting for me. I saw spines that were straightened, people breathing well who had been having a hard time breathing for a long time, I saw people walk who couldn't before, people leave wheelchairs, and many other things that the healing teams were ministering to.

One thrilling thing was to see the excitement and joy

of the healing teams when someone they were ministering to would be healed. At Lakeland, I saw the excitement of one of the teams when a person with no fingers got stubs growing out on a hand. You can just imagine the thrill they received when they ministered healing to someone for the first time in their lives and saw a healing.

I have been in the ministry for ten years and the Impossible Miracles Ministry got its start from a miracle I received at a Hunter meeting in Minneapolis on December 7, 1973. This ministry has been known as a healing ministry and I have received many other miracles. But the Healing Explosions I've seen this year topped them all. I was glad to be a supervisor at all of them and I look forward to many more Explosions.

Miraculously in Jesus,   Norma Jean LeRoy
(Dr. LeRoy's wife)

Thomas A. Owen, D.C., Ph.C, FAPC

My life was literally changed in one evening with the Charles and Frances Hunter healing ministry. First at a local church when my wife was healed of a thirty-two-year-old back problem. The next occurrence was my participation in a Healing Explosion where I found a tremendous amount of knowledge available through the Hunters, as well as the opportunity to share with the Hunters and the doctors and to participate in scores and scores of supernatural healings. So many unanswered medical voids are now being answered by this ministry that we doctors are founding a supernatural healing and research center in Jacksonville, Florida.

It's true! My life will never be the same — that's the standard experience of the "healer" and the "healee" at a Healing Explosion.   Thomas A. Owen

Dr. Pat Crotty, Chiropractor
God healed me through the Hunter's ministry! I needed it! I wanted it! But, I did not realize nor could I know that God would begin to do even more in my life!

In late October of 1985, I began to develop a severe pain in my left sacroiliac joint for no apparent reason. I am a practicing chiropractor of seven years standing and was able to quickly diagnose my problem. I had severely strained my left hip joint. Few people realize that chiropractors often develop back trouble themselves over years of treating their patients and long hours of bending over. In the ensuing weeks since my problem had occurred, the pain began to radiate into the acetabular cavity where the thigh bone joins the pelvic girdle. Walking became difficult and in time I began treating myself in my own office with both cold packs and ultrasound therapy. This gave me some relief, but walking was still very painful.

Eventually, I did what I knew I had to do, and that was to see a chiropractic colleague of mine. He did quite extensive kinesiology testing on me and found a separation and sprain of the sacroiliac ligament (he felt strongly that I may have damaged it). He also found a weakness of both the heart and pancreas, but could make no more of an exact diagnosis than that. I was not entirely surprised because, though I would not confess it with my mouth, I was exhibiting many of the symptoms of diabetes mellitus. Basically, I was tired all of the time, and felt totally drained of energy. I blamed it on a number of things...never taking time to rest, overwork, being overly fatigued mentally most of which wasn't true.

However, all of these were excellent reasons for avoiding what I didn't want to have done...a blood test or urinalysis! I was fearing the worst, of course. So, I began taking chiropractic treatments from my colleague friend, and they did help me. However, the pain would continue to come back which is rare for me, because I usually recover quickly from such things.

On another brief note, I need to share something of a personal nature that was going on inside of me for a long time, perhaps as long as a year. I began to feel very dissatisfied with my work which is strange because I love what I do for a living! But yet, something was missing and I was feeling less and less fulfilled. I prayed to the Lord for wisdom and guidance as to what He would have me to do. For a time I even felt maybe He had not really wanted me to be a chiropractor.

Well, by the end of November, 1985, I found out that Charles and Frances Hunter were going to be in Fargo, North Dakota (two hundred miles away from my area). Having heard so much about their wonderful ministry, I decided to attend their meeting.

At that meeting, over a thousand people received a healing touch from the Lord through Charles and Frances. People all over the place were praising God. Charles laid hands on me and my hip pain vanished. Then he said, "God is giving you a new heart and a new pancreas!" Praise God!

My hip pain left never to return. My energy level has increased 100% and I no longer feel tired! Thank You, Jesus! My colleague checked me and told me that everything was A-O.K., but it wasn't chiropractic that helped me, it was the healing power of God!!

Probably the biggest miracle of all was when the Hunters began to share God's vision of Healing Explosions and healing teams all across the nation, I knew in my spirit that this is what I had been searching for! God wanted to move me into *His* realm of healing and out of the realm of mortal man! I rejoice because deep within me I have always known I had a desire to touch people the way Jesus did, to see them be made well and whole.

I thank God so much for this ministry because it has changed my life and revitalized me as a Christian. I praise God and thank Him for Charles and Frances Hunter, two beautiful people who serve God with their whole heart. Pat Crotty, D.C.

by Charles and Frances
When you write a book like this one, it is almost impossible to find a stopping point. We just talked with Dr. Pat Crotty again. He didn't even go to a Healing Explosion, just to one service in North Dakota, and he just said, "I'll tell you something, MY LIFE HAS BEEN CHANGED!"

We sent him some of our books about healing and night before last he sat down and read "Don't Limit God". He was rather tired when he finished the day's work and the book, so he took his glasses off and took about a fifteen minute nap. When he got up, he put his glasses on and everything became blurry. He took them off and rubbed his eyes and they cleared up. He put the glasses back on and everything got blurry again. He tried to read a newspaper and couldn't.

He wondered if he had symptoms of diabetes or just what was going on. He picked up the newspaper again and without glasses the print was perfectly clear...even the fine print was easily readable! God had built his faith so much through reading the book that He just plainly healed his eyes and they have been perfect ever since.

He had attended two different churches for the last two years, both Spirit-filled, but was becoming discouraged with Pentecostal/Charismatics until he came to our service and saw Jesus alive and working like he had never seen before through two ordinary business people.

He attended a meeting of a group who are in Bible study about weight control as the Bible teaches it. One lady there said she had lumps in her breast and was afraid to go to a doctor, fearing the worst.

Dr. Crotty had just finished the first chapter of "To Heal the Sick", and with this little teaching he said, "Why don't we lay hands on you for healing?" He did and for the first time in his life, someone was slain in the Spirit. These people were not from a Spirit-filled church and they said, "What happened to her!"

We don't have the results of healing yet, but we believe as the power of God entered her body that she was healed. Why not, because it is the power of the Holy Spirit flowing from the Spirit of God within each of us that heals and that causes people to fall under the power.

His last few words blessed us as he shared his new life in power. He said he had never seen or felt such compassion and love as he felt in our meeting. We expressed to him that when God's healing team members, the believers, begin to do the works of Jesus by healing the sick and accompanying ministry, the compassion and love of Jesus begins to well up within them until they want to be a witness for Him!

Practicing Physician
Practices Divine Healing

Greetings in the words of the psalmist, David: "Bless the Lord, oh my soul: and all that is within me, Bless His holy name. Bless the Lord, Oh, my soul, and

forget not all of His benefits: Who forgiveth all thine in-
iquities; who healeth ALL thy diseases."

In the seventy-three years of my life, these past four
days have been the most exciting and stimulating days of
my life. I praise the Lord for all that we were taught, and
for the *faith* building experiences that we had there at
the Denver Healing Explosion. It was tremendous to see
what the Lord is doing even today and to learn and *know*
that this is the *norm* that God is expecting of believers
today. Hallelujah!! I shall never be the same. Now for
some of the experiences that the Lord shared through
me.

The first person to whom I ministered was during
our twelve-thirty noon break. He was an elderly man
who also was being taught for the team ministry. He
came and requested me to minister to him because his
eyes were failing. He had had cataract surgery in both
eyes several years ago, and because the left eye was totally unsuccessful, they had done a second surgery in this
left eye to put in a lens implant. This also had failed and
the vision in his right eye was also deteriorating. He
feared total blindness.

I thought, "What can I do?" So, I spoke for a short
time in tongues, and the Lord told me to lay my thumbs
on his eyes and speak the word of faith, recovery of his
sight and normalization of his vision. Before I was
finished speaking the words and commanding sight to
come back into those eyes, he went over in the power of
the Spirit. Our friend from Denver with whom we fel-
lowshipped a great deal and her husband caught him as
he went down.

The Lord did the healing because when he got up, he
looked around, held his hand over the right eye and said,
"I can see fairly clear with the left eye." Then he looked

with the right eye, and said happily, "I can see clearly." Praise the Lord, He was faithful, because I certainly had not felt that anything like that would happen.

The second one was a lady that also came to me while we were trying to eat lunch. She had a multitude of complaints. In fact, from her report, she was a physical wreck (speaking as a physician). My heart was not really in it because I was being disturbed in my lunch time. However, I began to speak healing to her problems and nothing happened. So, our friend, Mrs. Carlson, spoke to her problems and ministered to meet her needs, and she went over under the power of the Holy Spirit. As she arose, she testified that she felt so much better. I had been taught that when ministering in the name of, and in place of, the Lord Jesus Christ, eating lunch is not very important and can wait.

Then another man came by, and again requested ministry. He had a lot of joint and back pain, obviously arthritis. This time I looked to the Lord, spoke a few lines in the Spirit, and then felt led to cast out the demons of arthritis, and to speak healing to his back and joints. He too went down under the power of the Holy Spirit. When he arose, he testified that his pain was all gone, and he could move freely.

My next experience was our friend, the young dentist, who was also on the physicians' panel. After our afternoon session was over, he came to me and asked that I minister to his eyes. He is short-sighted, myopic, and asked that his vision be normalized. I again sought the Lord in tongues and He again showed me to lay my thumbs on the eyeballs. As I did this, I commanded the eyeballs to become more spherical and the focal point of vision to strike the retina in a perfectly spherical point so that the visual shortness would be gone.

He too went down under the power of the Holy Spirit. Fortunately, my wife had told our friend to go over to where we were and be catcher. He caught our dentist friend just in time to prevent him falling hard onto the chair that was a short distance behind him. When he arose, he looked around, held his hands close up to his face and way out, and said that he could see clearly. Then he looked up into the distance near the roof, and he could read the letters on the marquee scoreboard near the top of the back wall. He said that he had not been able to do this before. Praise the Lord.

I forgot to mention that the first gentleman to whom I ministered, the man with the cataracts...before speaking healing, his left eye not only had had two cataract surgeries, but also it was bulging out, exophthalmos. When he arose after healing was spoken to him, the eye was just as normal as the right eye...no longer bulging out.

In the evening service, my wife ministered to the first lady who had multiple sclerosis. I was the catcher, and it was exciting to see how faithfully the Lord responded to heal her. Dr. Owellen, the internist from Johns Hopkins, examined her afterwards, and he told the lady that her former drop foot was all gone and her leg would function normally.

The next lesson that I had to learn was the experience with the little lady from the Philippines. She had a left leg that was two-and-one-half inches shorter than the right. Another team had ministered to her and told her that she was healed and to go home "believing". My wife, Ella, saw her coming down the line very much discouraged and since she had met her at the hotel, she recognized her and spoke to her. She narrated her discouragement and disappointment in not being able to go home with a normal leg. So, my wife and I sat her down on the chair. My wife stood and interceded in tongues while I did the measuring, etc. It was obvious that even at the knee, the leg was two-and-one-half inches shorter than the right. Also, her muscles on the left leg had wasted considerably. I "thought" that she had had polio, and so I commanded the polio symptoms and weakness to leave, and the leg to grow out. It grew only about one-quarter of an inch, but NO MORE!

So I said: "Let's go to Charles and see what he will do." We went and she limped along with me.

I told Charles that I thought she had had polio, so after he had sat her down on the chair, he asked her, "Have you had polio?"

She said, "No, I had a broken hip." Then Charles had her stand up, laid his hands on her hips, and commanded the hip to go down and the bones to normalize and be healed. It was exciting to see his hand move down as that hip bone went down into position. Upon measuring, the leg was less than one-quarter of an inch shorter than the right leg. Praise the Lord, He did it again!!

I had learned that you do not speak to what you "think" they have, but you find out and ask "what the problem is" and then "speak to the problem and command it to change". I am glad I learned that . And I am glad and more so, that the lady was *healed*. Hallelujah!

After the last meeting on Saturday, we went with our friends, the Carlsons from Denver, and did a little shopping, then ate an early supper and went to our hotel room. We visited together for a while, and then Mrs. Carlson began narrating her physical problems and complaints. She had severe and distressing sinusitis which caused headaches; chronic asthma for which she frequently had to whiff a bronchodilator; plus severe backache from arthritis, etc. After a time we all got up and my wife sought the Lord in tongues, her husband stood behind her as catcher and I sought the Lord and then cursed those arthritis demons to come out of her body and commanded healing to the bones, joints, and connective tissues; commanded opening of the sinuses and normalizing of the mucous membranes of the nasal passages, the sinuses and throughout the lungs and commanded the air sacs in the lungs to open up; and also commanded the arteries and veins in her extremities to open up, and cholesterol to leave and normalize.

She went down under the power of the Spirit and her husband caught her. As she went down, her spine went B-R-R-R-R-R-R-R-R, all the way to the top. (I have never manipulated a back like that as an osteopath!)

She stayed down quite awhile, but the Lord did a *good job*! As she arose, she took a deep breath and said, "My lungs are open." After a bit she said, "My sinuses are clear. I can breathe. My headache is gone." As we asked her about her back, she shrugged her shoulders, bent over and said, "My stiffness and aching is gone." As we visited on and praised the Lord, all of a sudden she said, "My feet are warm!" Because of poor circulation, they had been cold for years. Hallelujah! God is faithful and just as true as His Word.

How tragic that the "church" lost this years ago. The world could have been evangelized years ago if the *living* Jesus had been demonstrated.

Richard F. Jantzen, M.D.

Nurse Georgie
After sitting under your teaching and reading your book "To Heal the Sick" and participating in the Healing Explosion, my life just hasn't been the same.

Jesus is saying, "Whom shall I send?" and I replied, "Here am I, Lord. Send me."

When I participated in the Healing Explosion, I wasn't in the wheelchair section and I didn't think that I saw any miraculous healings. I saw arms and legs grow out and people being healed of various back ailments. But because I didn't see what I really wanted to see, I let Satan torment me with thoughts of not being able to really be used to see the miraculous.

But praise the Lord, Jesus just quickened to my spirit Luke 10:19 and how He said, "Behold, I give unto you power to tread on serpents and scorpions, and over all the power of the enemy." (KJV) I said, "Yes, in the name of Jesus, I will go wherever you want me to go."

I work in a coronary care unit in a local hospital and I praise the Lord for what He has done. I have had a burden for the lost since I accepted Jesus Christ as my Savior, but I knew that there had to be more. Because of your teaching, I am so thankful of your act of mercy in going around the world; and because of what you have taught us, I now can say, "Yes, in the name of Jesus be healed!" and I just praise Him for what He has done.

Charles and Frances, as you share just what has happened in my life, and I know what is happening in so many others, and especially as you share this with medical personnel, I would like you to encourage them to get in touch with the Hospital Christian Fellowship. This is a worldwide organization, and their whole purpose is "to lead all of those in the hospital and health services to a saving knowledge of our Lord Jesus Christ and to encourage the deepening of their spiritual lives." This is an international organization and it is to help everyone who is involved in the medical field to reach out to people.

The hospitals are our pulpits and everybody in any

type of medical field needs to grab hold of your message today. More people go through the hospitals in a year than go through the churches.

I went back to work after that Healing Explosion all fired up and I said, "Oh, Lord, who do you want me to go to and where do you want me to go?" So many things have happened, but the most important story that I can share with you is about a man who had just gone through a cardiac arrest, and they rushed him into our unit, the coronary care unit.

We hurried and started our routine CCU orders. This man, I'll call him Bill, was practically dead. Normal blood pressure is 120 over 80, and the only thing we could get was 30 over palp. We opened dopamine, dobutrex, and levophed. We had just about every drug imaginable running into him.

Any nurse in the medical profession will understand that when you run these drugs, because they are so potent, it is only so many drops at a time. You figure out the microdrops and then calculate, but Bill was so critical that we were actually running these drugs into him as fast as they could get into him in order to maintain the little blood pressure he had.

He was intubated and on a respirator; but during this entire time, Bill was completely "alert" and during an "alert" situation in a hospital, you have many personnel involved. You have your EKG technician, your respiratory therapist, plus all of your doctors and nurses and the supervisors, so you have at least twenty people present during a life-threatening situation.

At this moment I felt completely compelled of the Lord to start praying for Bill. The Lord has given me a boldness through many ways that He has taught me. "Choose you this day whom you will serve" and because

I have made it my decision to serve Jesus, I have now learned obedience. So regardless of how many people were in the room, I said, "Bill, do you know Jesus Christ as your Lord and Savior," and he acknowledged that he did. He couldn't talk because he had an endotracheal tube down his throat, but he was completely awake and he shook his head. Despite everything we were doing, nothing was really happening. We could not maintain a blood pressure above thirty or forty millimeters.

We called his doctor at home. This was at two o'clock in the morning, and the doctor said there was nothing else that we could do, so we kept working with Bill. The doctors who were running the "alert" on him just kept saying, "Well, is he still alert?" They were just waiting to shut off the medication because they felt that it was totally hopeless. We called his family and asked them to please try to get in as soon as possible so that they could see him before he died.

I stood by that bed and kept praying over him, praying out loud and Bill just kept holding my hand and squeezing it. I was watching the monitor and said, "Oh, Lord, please keep him alive until his family gets in here." Finally, his family came in and they were concerned because his son was in Georgia and Bill wanted to see him. We were finally able to get in touch with the son and I said again, "Oh, Jesus, please keep him alive until the son comes in."

At one point as I was watching the monitor, Jesus said to me, "You go into that room and take authority over the spirit of death!"

I said, "Yes, sir, Jesus." I walked into that room and I said, "O.K., Bill, here I am again and this time we're going to pray, but we're not just going to pray now for a plain healing. We're going to pray for an absolute and total complete healing and you're going to get up out of this bed and you're going to walk out of this hospital. I just took authority over that spirit of death in the name of Jesus, I bound Satan in the name of Jesus and continued to pray over Bill throughout that night.

Before I'd gone in and taken authority over that spirit of death, the family had approached me about donating his organs. I had contacted the supervisor of the hospital, she contacted the donor bank. But, when she explained his condition and all of the medications that we were running into him, the donor bank said to please thank the family very much for their consideration in wanting to donate his organs, but he was too far gone and his organs really wouldn't be of use to anyone. They said about the only thing that they could do was to donate his eyes. I gave that message to the family and they were praying about whether or not his eyes should be donated.

I continued to pray for him throughout the night and when morning came, it was time for me to leave. I went home and continued to pray for him. When I came in the next night, his family was waiting for me. The son had arrived and the family just couldn't believe that Bill was still alive. I just praised the Lord.

Bill continued to get better, he got off the ventilator and when he would put his light on, he was not asking for pain pills or his sleeping pill but was saying, "I want my prayers!" Oh, hallelujah! He knew he was alive because of who Jesus Christ is. Jesus reached out and touched him.

Oh, saints, we just need to be obedient. Charles and Frances taught us to take authority over the spirit of death. Because Jesus said, "You go in and do it", I did it and this man was totally healed. He walked out of that hospital completely on his own, a case that they totally gave up on!

The nursing supervisor had been on vacation for a couple of weeks and when she came back, as soon as she saw me, she said, "Oh, by the way, did the family donate Bill's eyes?"

I said, "No, they decided that he needed them!" then I shared with her how he was miraculously healed! Thank You, Jesus! Oh, saints, we just need to be obedient to the calling of Christ!

A couple of weeks ago we had another patient "life-flighted" in from another hospital. On his way in, he "alerted" as they worked with him. I guess because of the amount of time that was involved before they were able to revive him, he was totally confused. Enough oxygen had not profused the brain by the time we got him and he was just like a vegetable. Then he was like a wild man and so we had to restrain him. The restraints were on just as tight as could be...his arms were tied down, his legs were tied down and we had a chest posey on him.

He remained in this condition for several days. I was assigned to take care of him one night. When I went in the room, I closed those doors and pulled that curtain and said, "All right, Satan, I've just had enough of your foolishness and I bind you in the name of Jesus Christ!" I took authority over that spirit of confusion and commanded it to loose this man in the name of Jesus. I put my hands on his brain and commanded those cells to be re-oxygenated in the name of Jesus.

I told this man that I wanted him to pray a prayer after me and I kept repeating it to him so that he would ask Jesus to come into his heart even though he didn't know what he was doing. With the authority that only Jesus Christ can give, I spoke to him and as he repeated that prayer, I told him to just keep saying, "Jesus, heal me, Jesus, heal me!"

He had dopamine running wide open into him and if that goes into the tissues, it is so potent that the tissues will turn black. Evidently, that is what happened. From his wrist down, his hand was totally black. They said "We'll just have to amputate it", but praise the Lord, I wouldn't accept that either. I continued to pray over the hand and the fingers.

Just a few days later I saw this man walking the halls and I said, "Hey, Jim, let me see your hand."

He showed it to me, and said, "Why, it's fine now." When I saw him, I just burst out in laughter over the joy of seeing a man who was a wild animal being strapped down in bed changed into a man who was up walking around with a hand that is completely healed! Glory! Hallelujah!

I had another patient, his name is Charles. He was completely healed of his diabetes. He had been in our unit before I went to the Healing Explosion. The Lord brought him back in and this time he wasn't having any problems with his heart. He didn't even know quite why he was in there, but he happened to mention to me that he was having a lot of problems with his diabetes. I said, "Well, we don't have to accept that!"

I received so much encouragement from you at the Healing Explosion when you said, "All right, everybody that hasn't received the baptism with the Holy Spirit stand up, and I never saw anybody do it that way before.

Others would say, "Well, if you want to receive...", sort of namby-pamby....but you said, "Just stand up..." and 5,000 people received the baptism of the Holy Spirit.

So Charles (my patient) is telling me about his diabetes, and I said, "Well, Charles, first of all, you need the baptism with the Holy Spirit." (I knew that Charles was saved because we had established that the first time he was in CCU.) "Do you know anything about it?" He said, "No, not really." So I shared the baptism with him and he just broke out in a beautiful prayer language and we stood there at that bedside and just praised the Lord in other tongues for about five minutes!

What an anointing was present and I said, "All right, Charles, are you ready to be delivered from this diabetes?" He was so ready and I took authority over that foul spirit of diabetes in the name of Jesus Christ and cast it out...and went on about my work that night.

A few nights later the Lord brought him back to my attention and inspired me to look up what his glucose was. I really hadn't thought anything more about it. I looked on the chart. His glucose was 112, and all nurses know that is a normal glucose. Then to prove his healing, I told Charles, "You ought to ask the doctor to do a two-hour post-parandial test or a glucose tolerance test so that we can have this documented."

Charles said he was kind of concerned. He had mentioned to the doctors that he didn't understand why he was getting trays now with cake, pie and ice cream. He kept saying to the doctor, "I'm a diabetic."

So the doctor went over his chart and ordered a two-hour post-parandial test which came back completely within normal limits. He said, "Charles, there is no way I can call you a diabetic. You are *not* a diabetic."

Charles had been taking medicine for years for his diabetes. In fact, he had just gotten all of his prescriptions filled before he came into the hospital this time. But he said, "I sure don't need them anymore!"

I encourage everyone, especially the medical profession, to please take this message to your patients and to the families who are in the hospital. The waiting rooms are filled with people who need the hope of the gospel of Christ. We can take this message everywhere, including our churches.

My husband and I have seen services in our church where members of the healing teams have been asked to come up and minister healing to the people. Bill and I have seen arthritis completely healed as we have taken authority over the spirit of arthritis. We have seen deaf ears opened as we have taken authority over the deaf spirits, and also many, many back ailments cured. So, no matter where Jesus is calling us to go... into the highways and byways...because of His faithfulness, we will go!

*Note: You may contact the Hospital Christian Fellowship at P.O. Box 4004, San Clemente, Ca 92672.

Dr. Harrison Prater

My first experience was the Lakeland Healing Explosion. It started out to be an educational one. I wanted to learn more about healing and I knew Charles and Frances Hunter were the leading authorities in this field and they could teach me what I didn't learn in any of the other colleges or universities I had been to in the past. After going through the most dynamic Spirit-filled classes that anyone could ever ask for, I soon learned what the Happy Hunters meant when they speak of "people healing people".

I drove down from Orlando, Florida to Lakeland every day, and the more I learned about healing, the more I felt the Spirit of the Lord leading me to do more than just sit and listen. So, I told the Lord if He wanted me to do more, to open the doors. Boy, did He ever! Frances Hunter asked if I would like to be on the panel of physicians, and that's where I received the biggest blessing of my life.

I saw people I would have diagnosed as terminal and cases that seemed totally hopeless for any possible cure that could be obtained medically by any conventional means. But as they filed upon the stage, I saw scoliosis, bladder problems, deafness and many pathological conditions healed right before my little scientific eyes. After re-examination of the same patients, they were, in fact, divinely and totally, I might add, HEALED!

I didn't realize it at the time, but the Lord had even bigger blessings just around the corner, and that was the night of the Healing Explosion itself. He had to prepare me so I could be used by Him the way I had asked Him to do, so He allowed the only thing I had doubts about to come directly to me that very day.

Frances was on stage and suddenly she said, "I feel a healing coming over this crowd and fillings are being put in people's mouths."

I'm ashamed to say that my faith wasn't at the level it should have been, and my first thought was, "Come on, Frances, really now!"

But that very evening, a lady came up to me for healing and I told her that I would love to do that for her, but I had promised someone else and I would be right back. She said, "That's O.K. I've waited two days to get to you, so ten to fifteen minutes more won't hurt."

I went to help these other people and when I was finished, I was getting ready for lunch. I walked around the church and I heard my name called again. And sure enough it was this very same lady who had been waiting two days, but now it was two days and two-and-one-half hours, but the wait was really worth it for me. She asked if I had forgotten her, and I apologized and admittedly said, "Yes!"

She said, "It doesn't matter — just lay hands on me now." So I did and she was healed and fell under the power of God. As she was getting up we were talking about her faith, and she said, "The other night as Frances was talking about fillings in people's teeth, I felt something warm against my tongue and the Lord told me it was a filling."

"Now," I thought, "I've got two of them! First, Frances, and now, her!"

Then the lady explained, "I said, 'Lord, if you are putting in fillings, just make it gold while You're at it.'"

Before I could doubt it any longer, this lady pulled her jaw back and right on the sidewalk I saw one of the prettiest gold teeth I have ever seen! It was so pretty I wanted a gold ring made out of it. At that very moment I knew that *ALL* things are possible with God and how even the fillings in people's mouths were important to Him and healings can take place anywhere in the body, including the mouth.

That was exactly what I needed to see because the night of the Healing Explosion, Frances asked the doctors on the healing panel to supervise the other healing teams for that evening. All that day Satan wanted to rob me of the blessings the Lord had in mind for me, and also a chance to be used by the Lord to help others with their healing, so he kept telling me I couldn't help that many and it was just impossible and that the Lord could not serve that many that easily, and a lot of other lies.

But the very moment I stepped out off of that stage and came close to each sick person, the only thing that I could see was that big new gold tooth right smack in the middle of my forehead like it was imprinted on my brain. Then I saw hearing restored, the lame walk, people with arthritis cured and even a man who had been run over by a Mack truck with his head literally on his chest, able to move only his eyes, and one missing leg with absolutely no movement or feeling in his leg. After directing the healing team what to speak "life" into, the man's head came up, he looked at us with a big smile and he started praising God.

I spoke life into his leg and he started moving it. I was so grateful to be on the healing staff because I had the opportunity of watching "healers" heal people and as I was pulled over to the very worst cases to help out with, I saw God's power move like I had never known before. So if you say I was in a life-changing experience with Jesus, your assumption would be 100 per-cent correct.

I only wish I had known Charles and Frances and their teachings before I studied medicine for ten-and-one-half years. How wonderful and how much easier it would have been because I learned *people can heal people,* and most of all, *Jesus is alive and well!*

Dr. Harrison Prater, D.C., M.S.,B.S.

P.S. I have led more people to the Lord since the revelations and experiences in the Healing Explosion than I ever have in my whole life, and I'm looking forward to more!

Chapter Fifteen

The Beginning of the End

As we have written this book to share with you the marvelous, wonderful miracles Jesus has done through the BELIEVERS we have trained for the Healing Explosions, we pray that you will see the vision God gave us about the end-time harvest coming true before your very eyes. This is just the beginning!

Never before have we been so excited and elated as we are about how God is opening this new, dynamic healing world to great multitudes of ordinary people. We truly believe this is but the beginning of the end-time harvest which will come before the return of Jesus.

A great and mighty sweep of the Holy Spirit came to the body of Christ during what was called the latter rain. There was some "wild-fire" along with this as some went into extremes of emotion, and some got well into the flesh in prophecy, interpretation and other gifts of the Spirit.

When you look at the extremes of any move of God, you can become uneasy that people might think everyone is like that, and so we are inclined to draw back from letting the Holy Spirit have His full freedom. We are told by some who have been in Pentecost much longer than we have that many quenched the Spirit just to preserve order.

God is sweeping mightily in the training and activating of the ministry of healing by ordinary believers through these great and wonderful Healing Explosions. He is using even some whom we might think of as "flakes" and some who seem not to listen to their instructions. Some seem to say people are healed when that is just an assumption. Some may give "prophecies" or "words of knowledge" when it is their own imagination or their own desires of what should happen.

We learned long ago to look at the ones who are healed and not the ones who are not. We look for the healing, not the sickness. We look for the absence of pain, not what's left of the pain. We thank Jesus when even ten percent or fifty percent of the pain leaves, and when we praise Him for what He *has* done, we see that faith in action brings the completion of the healings.

When and if you see someone who seems "out of line" or "in the flesh" or "not following the instructions" we gave, just "exactly like we gave them", just know that Jesus did not limit the believers or classify them as to flakes, emotional extremes, or highly qualified believers. He simply said when believers laid hands on the sick that they would recover.

We believe the Holy Spirit is capable of handling all those who might not be quite like we would like for them to be. He is the One by whose power all healings are accomplished, and how we praise Jesus that whether or not they are "perfect", Jesus will be delighted when *any* believer is doing their best to please Him by doing *His* works!

As we looked back at the vision given to Frances and the one given to Tommy Hicks as quoted in our book "To Heal the Sick", we were astounded at the speed and accuracy of the fulfillment of those visions through the Healing Explosions.

As you read a portion of Frances' vision, note that we saw then what God is doing now. We referred to the City of Light School of Ministry, and this is now totally video, but is the very heart of the teachings for the Healing Explosions along with the book "To Heal the Sick".

"In June of 1980, God gave us a vision of the world with silver and gold bands covering the entire globe— but not in the orderly sense you would expect to see them. These bands were spilling all over the world like melted silver and gold rivulets and running into all sorts of odd little places — mountains and valleys alike There was no obvious plan of any kind represented by these silver and gold rivulets — they went hither and thither all over the place. Sometimes they were wide, and sometimes they were super skinny. In some places it looked like a big blob of melted silver and gold had fallen, but there was no pattern of any kind! Then we saw students begin to rise up and stand on these melted silver and gold bands.

We began to ponder on this, because in the beginning it seemed to us like nothing but a huge hodge-podge, but slowly God began to reveal what this vision meant, and how it applied to our ministry.

The more we examined this divine vision, the more we began to understand that God was telling us to take the total message of salvation, which includes healing, to the entire world, by letting the masses learn how to operate in the supernatural and heal the sick.

Our hearts began to sing as God continued the revelation of what He wanted us to do. First, He directed us to teach on the subject of "How To Heal The Sick". We had seen students from the City of Light School of Ministry standing on the silver and gold bands, and thought momentarily that they were going to go to all parts of the world to teach the nationals how to heal the sick. Somehow this understanding did not give us total assurance that this was actually what the vision meant. We continued to think more about the vision.

Then the picture expanded even more, and we saw the video schools going into ALL the world — into the small places where evangelists never go, to teach all the people in the remotest places of the world how to lay hands on the sick and heal them. The students who learned from these video tapes would then go out and preach the gospel to the poor, heal the broken-hearted, preach deliverance to the captives and recovering of sight to the blind, and set at liberty those who are bruised.

For the first time, we plainly saw the identity of the students standing on the bands! We had seen students of all nationalities, but had thought they would be coming to the school here in Texas. Then we realized they were the ones we might not ever meet, the ones who might only see us through video tapes, but the ones who had received the message of how to heal the sick and had gone out to stretch forth their hands to the sick!

This is God's timing for another great move of his Spirit as the masses are being trained to go out and minister on a one-to-one basis.

We were confident that God had opened our spirits to a dynamic, far-reaching mission of teaching the masses how simple it is to become a miracle-working disciple like those in the book of Acts.

As we reviewed these first three Healing Explosions and shared in this book some of the mighty acts of the disciples of the twentieth century, we saw the reality of the Tommy Hicks' vision. What a glorious church Jesus is developing as He begins to purify the lives of believers through the baptism with fire to rid ourselves of the old carnal nature which defends and pleases self, and replace it with the nature of Jesus which has a life-giving compassion to do the works the Father sent Him and us to do.

As we have watched the ordinary believers in the body of Christ move into action in the arenas, we beheld this liquid light flow from their hands just as Tommy Hicks saw in his vision some twenty-five years before.

Look at just a summary of this mighty vision of the end-time ministry of ordinary people, and see the fulfillment appearing before our very eyes:

"The greatest thing that the church of Jesus Christ has ever been given lies straight ahead. It is so hard to help men and women to realize and understand the thing that God is trying to give to His people in the end-times...

"God is going to take the do-nothings, the nobodies, the unheard-ofs, the no-accounts. He is going to take every man and every woman and He is going to give to them this outpouring of the Spirit of God...

"Suddenly I beheld what looked like a great giant (the body of Christ)...And from these clouds suddenly there came great drops of liquid light raining down upon this mighty giant...

"Liquid drops of light began to flood the very earth itself and as I watched this giant that seemed to melt, suddenly it became millions of people over the face of the earth. As I beheld the sight before me, people stood up all over the world! They were lifting their hands and they were praising the Lord...

"Suddenly I saw a figure in white, in glistening white — the most glorious thing that I have ever seen in

my entire life. I did not see the face, but somehow I knew it was the Lord Jesus Christ, and He stretched forth His hand, and as He did, He would stretch it forth to one, and to another, and to another. And as He stretched forth His hand upon the nations and the people of the world — men and women — as He pointed toward them, this liquid light seemed to flow from His hands into them, and a mighty anointing of God came upon them, and those people began to go forth in the name of the Lord...

"As they marched forth in everything they did as the ministry of Christ in the end-times, these people were ministering to the multitudes over the face of the earth. Tens of thousands, even millions seemed to come to the message of the kingdom, of the coming kingdom, in this last hour.

"God is going to give to the world a demonstration in this last hour as the world has never known. These men and women are of all walks of life, degrees will mean nothing. I saw these workers as they were going over the face of the earth. When one would stumble and fall, another would come and pick him up. There were no "big I" and "little you", but every mountain was brought low and every valley was exalted, and they seemed to have one thing in common — there was a divine love, a divine love that seemed to flow forth from these people as they worked together, and as they lived together. It was the most glorious sight that I have ever known. Jesus Christ was the theme of their life...

"What a sight I had beheld! I had seen the end-time ministries — the last hour... My life has been changed as I realized that we are living in that end-time, for all over the world God is anointing men and woman with this ministry."

Jesus Christ is coming soon! Half of the world has never heard of Him. How are we going to get the most people saved, baptized with the Holy Spirit and out witnessing to the unbelievers? We must accomplish this massive world outreach to ignite *EVERY CHRISTIAN* to get out and do the works of Jesus.

The church age began with signs and wonders following the ordinary believers, and it will end in the same way — with mighty signs and wonders following ALL believers!

Jesus sent seventy men out to tell the people in the villages and towns that He would be coming soon. Jesus, we believe, is sending thousands of healing teams out today to tell the lost that He is coming soon, preparing their hearts to receive Him!

The Pittsburgh Healing Explosion was not just another meeting. It was an *explosion* which started on July 4, 1985, and will *END WITH THE RETURN OF JESUS!*

For further information about:

HEALING EXPLOSIONS -
When, where, what...
VIDEO HEALING SCHOOLS -
How to have your own...
CATALOG AND PRICE LIST -
Books, video and audio tapes by
Charles and Frances...

WRITE TO:

CHARLES ♥ FRANCES HUNTER
201 McClellan Road
Kingwood, Texas 77339 U.S.A.